DIRTY BOMB:

WEAPON OF MASS DISRUPTION

Gilbert King

Chamberlain Bros.
a member of
Penguin Group (USA) Inc.

DIRTY BOMB:

WEAPON OF MASS DISRUPTION

Chamberlain Bros.
A member of
Penguin Group (USA) Inc.
375 Hudson Street
New York, NY 10014

An application has been submitted to register this book with the Library of Congress.

Printed in the United States of America

1 3 5 7 9 10 8 6 4 2

This book is printed on acid-free paper. ∞

Book designed by Mike Rivilis.

TABLE OF CONTENTS

Prologue: New Year's Eve January 1, 2004 3

Introduction 9

Editor's Note. 15

1: What is a Dirty Bomb? 19

2: How Much Expertise Does It Take
   to Make a Dirty Bomb?. 25

3: What's The Difference Between
   a Nuclear Bomb and a "Dirty Bomb?" 29

4: Possible Types of Bombs
   and Delivery Methods. 41

5: Closer Than You Think. 67

6: The Effects of A Dirty Bomb Attack 83

7: What to Do in Case of a Dirty Bomb 91

8: How to Prevent a Dirty Bomb. 121

9: Dirty Secrets, Dirty Bombs: U.S. And Russia 133

Appendix
   1. List of Nuclear Facilities Around the World 143
   2. List of Acronyms. 163
   3. Glossary 165

Endnotes. 173

"It turned out that the locker belonged to a
homeless man and, tucked inside his duffel bag,
was a cigar-sized radium pellet, used to treat
uterine cancer. He had found it three years before."

– John Mintz and Susan Schmidt

PROLOGUE

NEW YEAR'S EVE, JANUARY 1, 2004

In Las Vegas on December 29, a homeless man was interrogated for five hours.

Police officials and government scientists and investigators hammered away at the struggling, mentally challenged man who proclaimed he had no idea that the cigar-shaped radium pellet, which is used in the treatment of cancer, was a potent radioactive sample. It was discovered at a self-storage warehouse, and the White House was immediately notified. "It turned out that the locker belonged to a homeless man and, tucked inside his duffel bag, was a cigar-sized radium pellet, used to treat uterine cancer. He had found it three years before," John Mintz and Susan Schmidt wrote in the Washington Post. Eventually, with the pellet confiscated, he was later released. But why the commotion? And was there a connection to the upcoming holiday?

There is no more famous a sight in the mind's eye than that of huge crowds of deliriously happy people bidding farewell to the old year and welcoming in the new one on any given New Year's Eve. With revelers huddled in giant throngs of shouting, bell-clanging, horn-blowing, air-horn-blasting joy, they eagerly wait in anticipation of the final countdown and all that the happy moment represents. Certainly the site of Times Square, delirious with partying New Yorkers, freshly frisked by police due to the heightened alert, were among those that come to mind.

Maybe the eve of December 31, 2003, was a naive night. As the world had finally put behind it the fall of the Taliban in Afghanistan and the fall of Iraq, it might have been for many the first time when Westerners were beginning to lose some of the apprehensions still haunting them from the terrible visions of 9/11.

However, that was not in fact the truth. Inserted into these celebrating, massive crowds, nervously clutching walkie-talkies and anxiously working with local authorities, scientists dispatched by the U.S. government were secretly watching. This was no mere study. They were looking for terrorists. "Casually dressed scientists concealed detection equipment in golf bags and briefcases while they looked for evidence of the bombs."

In fact, the government had suspected as early as December 19, 2003, that there might be a grave danger. On that day, when the government declared that the alert had been raised to its highest level, "The Homeland Security Department sent out hundreds of radiation monitors to police in Washington, New York, Los Angeles, Las Vegas, Chicago, Houston, San Diego, San Francisco, Seattle and Detroit," reported the *Washington Post*, which ran an AP report on

January 7, 2004. These devices are also known a radiation pagers. More than a thousand were distributed to those cities, as well as to police in Atlanta and Houston because of the expected large New Year's Eve crowds in those cities. "Batches of radiation pagers were also flown to authorities monitoring festivities at the Rose Bowl in Pasadena, California, and the Sugar Bowl in New Orleans.

"Department of Energy radiation experts were also dispatched to five cities to covertly look for evidence of a 'dirty bomb.' Beginning on December 22, the teams of scientists took measurements in the cities 24 hours a day," the newspaper went on to report. The Department also "sent a bulletin to local law enforcement agencies warning that detonating a dirty bomb was 'a top al Qaeda objective," reported ABC News on the same day as the *Post*, that cities with large ports like Baltimore, New York, Long Beach, and others, or those with large bridges with high traffic volumes such as the George Washington Bridge and the Golden Gate, were being monitored by Coast Guard patrols, equipped to detect even the lowest levels of radiation.

Why all this worry suddenly about dirty bombs? Where would they get such a device? And why would they strike now? The truth was, according to ABC, that the government was more than well aware of the threat of such a nuclear incident. In November 2003, "government investigators had documented 1,300 cases of lost, stolen, or abandoned radioactive material inside the U.S. over the past five years." With that kind of loss of control, it was easy to understand how government scientists and officials could be so worried about such a threat.

Secretary of State Colin Powell said in an ABC News Nightline interview, "I don't know how likely it is that there's a radiological weapon somewhere in the country. But if we know how to guard against that by disseminating around the country, nuclear scientists who have the wherewithal to monitor and measure, then that's the prudent step to take."

But the arrest of the homeless man was more important than most news watchers understood. The incident, however harmless it might appear, made it painfully clear that we now live in an age where the average citizen is at risk. The closer officials and reporters looked here at home, the more it became apparent that radioactive materials were in fact easily and readily available. Maybe not weapons-grade plutonium, but certainly radioactive waste. And it also became clear that unless steps were taken immediately, the threat of a dirty bomb wouldn't remain just a threat. The United States government was no longer treating dirty bombs as a matter of if, but of when.

"If al-Qaeda were to put together a
radiological device, they're going to use it."

– Cofer Black

INTRODUCTION

"A stick of cobalt, an inch thick and a foot long, is taken from among hundreds of such sticks at a food irradiation plant. It is blown up with just 10 pounds of explosives in a 'dirty bomb' at the lower tip of Manhattan, with a one-mile-per-hour breeze blowing. Some 1,000 square kilometers in three states is contaminated, and some areas of New York City become uninhabitable for decades."
—Nicholas D. Kristoff, A Nuclear 9/11, New York Times, March 10, 2004

The governments of Afghanistan and Iraq may have been overthrown, but they were not the haymakers that White House policymakers hoped they might be in the war against the terrorists. And while Osama bin Laden may be in hiding, it is no secret he and Al Qaeda view a nuclear strike against the United States as the ultimate weapon of terror.

While newspapers carry stories about dirty bombs from time to time few readers know enough about these bombs to be scared. And scared they should be. The threat of a nuclear strike is more real than ever, and the government, while trying to do its best, is playing from way behind. Some experts even wonder if we should be spending less money on trying to prevent it, and more on trying to deal with one after it happens.

The United States is not a secure country. First, our borders with Canada and Mexico are not secure, with thousands of miles of demarcated yet unguarded wilderness, an easy route for transporting a preassembled bomb. And with thousands of miles of coastline, the Navy, the Coast Guard, and the Air Force have not been able to stop the flow of rumrunners, drug smugglers, and illegal immigrants for almost a century now, let alone gunrunners and weapons brokers. Over the past five years, there have been thousands of cases documented where various kinds of radioactive materials have been found. And while terrorists may not have been able to get their hands on enough plutonium for a nuclear explosion, there is still enough around to make a low-grade but nonetheless effective dirty bomb.

Outside of the United States, in places like the former Soviet Union, Western Europe, Asia, Africa, and the Middle East, it is a veritable shopkeeper's bazaar of nuclear trinkets. The list of missing and discarded atomic energy production parts, radioactive medical waste, and other salvaged material make even the most staunch individuals weak in the knees.

And while the government is doing its best to seek out Al Qaeda operatives in the United States and keep their nefarious barbarian brethren from breaking down our gates, there are too many loopholes in our free and open society for them not to get through.

With the assistance of rogue states, corrupt officials, and terrorist operatives, it is inevitable that at the very least a dirty bomb, if not a nuclear weapon, will be unleashed by a terrorist operation, on an unsuspecting urban population sometime in the near future. It may or may not be on U.S. soil, but gone are the days that one could say with impunity, "It'll never happen here."

When the Twin Towers fell, so fell away our innocence, our naiveté. As the memory of 9/11 recedes, and the pace of everyday life reasserts itself, it is important to not lose sight that this global village we live in is much smaller than it was forty years ago when small renegade terrorist groups terrorized Europe, Asia, and the Middle East. In the Twenty-first century, the local internet café provides a chat room for those who would blow up your life, the local hospital dumpster provides the material for making the bomb, and the airline provides the target.

However, we must also face facts. While it was Iran that detonated the first dirty bomb, Arabs the world over are quick to point out that the United States and Soviet Union have been dropping depleted uranium bombs on military and civilian targets for more than a decade. Even today, there are reports from our European allies of sites a decade old where depleted uranium bombs – in effect, dirty bombs filled with TNT (which is lethal even before detonation) and radioactive isotopes - have poisoned the Middle Eastern landscape for the next thousand years. Who will clean these places up? the Arabs ask. Surely, the dissatisfaction and anger that feeds Al Qaeda's warped ranks comes from this inequity, but that is the business of nations, maybe even the Hague. It is not up to a group of fanatics to seek revenge by terrorizing the whole world with its own idea of racial, religious, and political purity.

"Al-Qa`ida continues to pursue its strategic goal of obtaining a nuclear capability. It remains interested in dirty bombs. Terrorist documents contain accurate views of how such weapons would be used," said CIA director George Tenet before the Senate Select Committee on Intelligence on February 24, 2004. Al Qaeda has the technology and the will.

As Mr. Tenet went on to say in his Senate testimony, "The continuing threat remains clear. Al-Qa'ida is still dedicated to striking the U.S. homeland, and much of the information we've received in the past year revolves around that goal." One alleged conspirator has been detained who has tried to secure the materials necessary in building such a bomb. Al Qaeda is like a surgeon probing with a scalpel, looking for the right area, before plunging its knife in fully. It may not be today or tomorrow, but they have numerous operatives operating under the radar. Another will probe in a different place, and another still in a different place. They will continue to mine this information, just as they have in the past, until they are successful, or until our government brings them down.

As recently as February 8, 2004, U. S. Ambassador-at-Large Cofer Black told the Associated Press, "If al-Qaeda were to put together a radiological device, they're going to use it. We know that they have the determination, they've killed large numbers before, their objective is to kill more, they're doing everything they can to acquire this type of weapon and we are working to try to prevent it."

But the technology and understanding of what is possible was best illustrated by an event that took place in Moscow in 1996. In that city's Izmailovo Park, police were alerted to an undetonated dirty bomb made with a container of caesium 137, which was taken from hospital radiation equipment, wrapped in explosives planted by Chechen rebels. It was the rebels who told police where it was. The bomb was never activated, so local authorities were spared the dubious first. But it very clearly counters those people who say building a dirty bomb is so dangerous that it is highly unlikely.

"The package contained…caesium 137 a highly radioactive material which, if it had been released into the atmosphere, could have contaminated thousands of people," reported Hamish Robertson for ABC News.

The threat of a dirty bomb is very real, and its effects have been reassessed. While it has only the destructive force of a conventional bomb, it will achieve the ultimate success as both a scare weapon and a weapon aimed more against our fortress economy than against our fortress walls. The clouds of radioactive fallout from a few of these "dirty bombs" may just yet be powerful enough to bring down the greatest single economy the world has ever seen, and drag down with it the rest of the Western world as we know it.

EDITOR'S NOTE

Some may say that this book is nothing more than sensationalism, or, at worst, scaremongering, complaining that it plays off the worst fears we all harbor deep down inside. We would hardly disagree. But it also is meant to inform, identify, and place in perspective the scenarios that have been bandied about since 9/11.

The dirty bomb scenario is the monster in the closet we don't want to admit to each other we see each night when we shut off the lights. But this is no fairy-tale creature from childhood. The dirty bomb threat is very real and imminent.

Should we all stay ignorant, then, and hide our fears and not talk about it? That would seem as silly as saying, "If you pay no attention to it, it will go away." It would be akin to Neville Chamberlain's appeasement miscalculation, more than 65 years ago. We cannot bury our heads in the sand like the ostrich. This is no terrorist cookbook. Instead, it is the real and factual truth about what we know right now, about what we can do if it happens and what we need to consider to prevent it.

Do we do what our parents and grandparents did when the atomic age was foisted upon them and build bomb shelters to wait out a nuclear winter that could last decades? A much more thoughtful response is needed. We have enough nuclear weapons to blow the world up several, times over. Do we disregard the facts surrounding nuclear weapons? Or do we face this threat now, courageously and smartly?

The dirty bomb is meant both as a weapon of terror and disruptive threat. It is scary, and those who would use it against us mean to scare us. But we can and must triumph over it.

One cannot cite a better quote than that of Michael Krepon, founder of the Henry L. Stimson Center think tank, when he told a U.S. Senate committee, "The first act of nuclear terrorism will be a momentously bad event."

"The first act of nuclear terrorism

will be a momentously bad event."

– Michael Krepon

CHAPTER 1:

WHAT IS A DIRTY BOMB?

"Osama bin Laden has made no secret of his ambition to join the nuclear club - he has even proclaimed it a 'religious duty' for Muslim states to acquire nuclear, chemical and biological weapons to attack the West, wrote Tony Karon for *Time* magazine in November 2001. However, Karon and *Time* confirmed that bin Laden has only achieved "a limited membership of that club, in the form of radioactive material that could be dispersed using conventional explosives – the so-called 'dirty bomb.'"

It became a very real scenario when the *Times of London* had also reported in November, Karon pointed out, that "Western intelligence officials believe bin Laden's organization has acquired nuclear materials, allegedly from Pakistan." Pakistan vehemently denied these reports, but other authorities have confirmed it. The International Atomic Energy Agency also signaled an alert, somewhat earlier, claiming, "We have been alerted to the potential of terrorists targeting nuclear facilities or using radioactive sources to incite panic, contaminate property, and even cause injury or death among civilian populations."

A dirty bomb is also known as a "Radiological Dispersal Device" (RDD). It is, in essence, as simple a device as possible, and very cheap by most standards. Essentially, it "is a conventional explosive such as dynamite that has been packed with radioactive material, which scatters when the bomb goes off. A dirty bomb kills or injures through the initial blast of the conventional explosive and by airborne radiation and contamination," reported the Council on Foreign Relations

The explosives could range from the traditional dynamite, to TNT (otherwise known as trinitrotoluene), to a fertilizer bomb, or to any other series of crude bombs described in numerous U.S. Army manuals up through the mid-1980s.

"High explosives inflict damage with rapidly expanding, very hot gas. The basic idea of a dirty bomb is to use the gas expansion as a means of propelling radioactive material over a wide area rather than as a destructive force in its own right. When the explosive goes off, the radioactive material spreads in a sort of dust cloud, carried by the wind, that reaches a wider area than the explosion itself," wrote Tom Harris for howstuffworks.com.

"At the levels created by most probable sources, not enough radiation would be present in a dirty bomb to kill people or cause severe illness. For example, most radioactive material employed in hospitals for diagnosis or treatment of cancer is sufficiently benign that about 100,000 patients a day are released with this material in their bodies," claimed the U.S. Nuclear Regulatory Commission.

"However, certain other radioactive materials, dispersed in the air, could contaminate up to several city blocks, creating fear and possibly panic and requiring potentially costly cleanup," the commission continued. "A second type of RDD might involve a powerful radioactive source hidden in a public place, such as a trash receptacle in a busy train or subway station, where people passing close to the source."

"Dirty nukes are what you may choose to build if you're unable to create a real nuclear bomb, i.e., one whose explosion is based on a nuclear reaction," wrote Mark Thompson, *Time* Pentagon correspondent. "The military usefulness of such devices have always been in dispute. In fact, the TNT in such a bomb may still be more dangerous than the nuclear material."

Intelligence officials have deduced that it is far easier and far more likely a terrorist organization will attempt to detonate a dirty bomb rather than just a conventional explosion. Its power will not be enough to kill, say, "10,000 people, but any bomb that killed people and set off Geiger counters would terrify a whole city," Thompson reported.

And it rightly should. The real affects of the dirty bomb have been hotly debated. Depending on the intensity of the radiating particles, the results could be quite debilitating for any densely populated urban area. "The long-term destructive force of the bomb would be ionizing radiation from the radioactive material. Ionizing radiation, which includes alpha particles, beta particles, gamma rays and X-rays, is radiation that has enough energy to knock an orbital electron off of an atom," Tom Harris reported.

This is the idea of the dirty bomb, to create a situation where radiation would affect the local population long after the explosion. If ions are released in the body, the effects can be serious. Basically, according to Harris, "an ion's electrical charge may lead to unnatural chemical reactions inside cells. Among other things, the charge can break DNA chains. A cell with a broken strand of DNA will either die or the DNA will develop a mutation."

Cell death can cause the body to break down, making it susceptible to diseases. Mutation can lead to cancer. When numerous cells all begin to fail at once, the result is also known as radiation sickness. People can survive radiation sickness, but usually thanks to a bone marrow transplant.

As a people, we are exposed to radiation every day. Many patients leave hospitals with radiation still affecting their systems. But all of these exposures are at fairly low levels, and their affects are so minimal we fail to see their effect. The tactical effect of the dirty bomb from the military's point of view, and from the point of view of the terrorist as well, is that a successful dirty bomb would raise the radiation levels well above normal. While it might not kill you the day it explodes, it will get you "years down the road," if you stay in the area.

"The extent of local contamination would depend on a number of factors, including the size of the explosive, the amount and type of radioactive material used, and weather conditions," reported the U.S. Nuclear Regulatory Commission. "Prompt detectability of the kind of radioactive material employed would greatly assist local authorities in advising the community on protective measures, such as quickly leaving the immediate area, or going inside until being further advised. Subsequent decontamination of the affected area could involve considerable time and expense."

"Any bomb that killed people and set off

Geiger counters would terrify a whole city."

– Mark Thompson

CHAPTER 2:

HOW MUCH EXPERTISE DOES IT TAKE TO MAKE A DIRTY BOMB?

The making of a dirty bomb is relatively simple. It requires just the knowledge of basic bomb building, which is readily available. "No special assembly is required; the regular explosive would simply disperse the radioactive material packed into the bomb. The hard part is acquiring the radioactive material, not building the bomb," reported the Council on Foreign Relations. As early as March 2002, the *Washington Post* reported that the Bush administration had already assumed that Osama bin Laden's terrorist "network probably had such often-stolen radioactive contaminants as strontium 90 and cesium 137, which could be used to make a dirty bomb."

The reason that the dirty bomb is such an imminent threat is because of the ease of making it. "If terrorists wanted to build a radiological – or so-called dirty bomb – in America, they might very well start their search for materials in your own scrap metal yards," reported Jim Stewart of CBS News. However, one dirty bomb is not as dangerous as another. Depending on the amount and radiation levels of the particles included, the Council on Foreign Relations concluded, "We don't know if terrorists could handle and detonate high-grade radioactive material without fatally injuring themselves first."

"From medical devices to mechanical gauges using cesium, to food irradiation facilities using cobalt, there are more than 18,000 sources of industrial radiation in America," reported Jim Stewart. But while finding enough highly radioactive parts remains the second most easy part of building a dirty bomb, it is the last two parts that remain the most difficult.

Retrieving such parts is the second-hardest part. Finding them and carrying them exposes terrorists out on the largest scavenger hunt in history to potentially massive, and therefore deadly, amounts of radiation. In many cases, those who did not suffer severe radiation sickness would probably die anyway.

The hardest part is assembling the bomb. Making the bomb, as was discussed earlier, is easy, but it's the exposure of the bomb maker that is tremendously risky. In fact, it would almost certainly be a suicide mission. "To make an effective one you need a lot of radioactive material – which either means making a shield so heavy the bomb becomes impossible to move – or building a bomb without a shield," Stewart concluded, "which would mean almost instant death." And the Council on Foreign Relations agrees, stating, "We don't know if terrorists could handle and detonate high-grade radioactive material without fatally injuring themselves first."

"Radiological attacks constitute a credible threat.
Radioactive materials that could be used for such
attacks are stored in thousands of facilities around
the U.S., many of which may not be adequately
protected against theft by determined terrorists."

– Henry Kelly

CHAPTER 3:

WHAT'S THE DIFFERENCE BETWEEN A NUCLEAR BOMB AND A DIRTY BOMB?

"A dirty bomb is the type of weapon you would build if you could not construct a conventional nuclear device," reported Dr. David Whitehouse for the BBC in June of 2002. "It would be messy but effective for many reasons."

However, a dirty bomb and a nuclear weapon are two different things. The costs to build a nuclear bomb require vast resources of wealth and materials few nations can muster, let alone a terrorist organization, however successful it may be.

The Bulletin of the *Atomic Scientist* reported, "Producing either uranium-235 or plutonium-239 in the quantities needed to make nuclear weapons is extraordinarily difficult and expensive. [Nuclear-bomb makers] must be prepared to spend hundreds of millions of dollars, or even billions."

"Operating a nuclear program would be a Herculean challenge for an organization whose survival depends on its relative invisibility," wrote Tony Karon for *Time*. As he pointed out quite saliently, "Even fully-functioning states such as Pakistan have needed decades of research and the assistance of nuclear-capable allies to develop their bomb programs." And Pakistan didn't have to hide their vast network of scientists and laboratories, and make sure those weapons were transportable.

The explosion in a nuclear device involves a complex nuclear fission or fusion reaction. In a nuclear bomb, the explosion is the means of mass destruction. And its results can level a whole city, or destroy part of a city but kill all its inhabitants nonetheless.

HIROSHIMA AND NAGASAKI

To understand the difference in technology and capability of a nuclear bomb as opposed to a dirty bomb, lessons in history and physics are required. In the history of recorded human affairs, atomic bombs have been used only twice in warfare as an act of aggression toward another country. In both instances, it was the United States that detonated those bombs and Japan was the target. The first and most important blast site is Hiroshima. A bomb made of uranium, which weighed more than four-and-a-half tons (nicknamed "Little Boy"), was dropped on Hiroshima on August 6, 1945. The Aioi Bridge, one of eighty-one bridges connecting the seven-branched delta of the Ota River, in Hiroshima, was the bull's-eye of the bomb, and ground zero was set at 1,980 feet. At 0815 hours, the bomb was dropped from the Enola Gay. It missed by only 800 feet. At 0816 hours, in the flash of an instant, 66,000 people were killed and 69,000 people were injured by the ten-kiloton atomic explosion.

The point of total vaporization from the blast measured a half mile in diameter. Total destruction measured one mile. Severe blast damage measured two miles. At two and a half miles, everything flammable burned. The remaining area of the blast zone was riddled with serious blazes that stretched out at a little over three miles.

On August 9, 1945, the second explosion, a plutonium bomb nicknamed "Fat Man," was dropped on the city of Nagasaki. Even though the bomb missed its target by over a mile and a half, it still leveled nearly half the city. Nagasaki's population dropped instantly from 422,000 to 383,000: 39,000 were killed, and more than 25,000 were injured. The blast was less than ten-kilotons as well. Estimates from physicists who have studied both explosions state that the bombs utilized only one-tenth of one percent of their respective capabilities.

A FISSION BOMB

"There are two main types of nuclear weapons: atom bombs which use fission as the main reaction, i.e. the atoms are split; hydrogen bombs which use fusion as the main reaction, i.e. the atoms are fused together," according to Alyn Ware, coordinator of the Parliamentary Network for Nuclear Disarmament. The two bombs dropped on Japan were fission bombs. These are the easiest bombs to re-create.

The two easiest processes to recreate are the enrichment of uranium and plutonium. Those are the two that intelligence agents are more concerned about. The hydrogen bomb is too complex for a terrorist network to even consider. Mining, extracting, and processing uranium and plutonium are painstakingly difficult, very expensive, and require lots of highly technical equipment. Uranium is highly radioactive, and is also unstable, meaning its atoms decay over time. It is this decay that causes the release of energy and radiation.

"Uranium-235 is very difficult to extract," according to outlawlabs.com. "In fact, for every 25,000 tons of Uranium ore that is mined from the earth, only 50 tons of Uranium metal can be refined from that, and 99.3% of that metal is U-238 which is too stable to be used as an active agent in an atomic detonation. To make matters even more complicated, no ordinary chemical extraction can separate the two isotopes since both U-235 and U-238 possess precisely identical chemical characteristics. The only methods that can effectively separate U-235 from U-238 are mechanical methods."

First gaseous diffusion is used to separate the two isotopes. Then the uranium is refined once again, using a magnetic separation process. Finally, a third enrichment process is applied. Once these procedures have been completed, all that needs be done is to place the properly molded components of uranium 235 inside a warhead that will facilitate an atomic detonation. Supercritical mass for uranium 235 is defined as 110 pounds (50 kgs) of pure uranium.

"Depending on the refining process(es) used when purifying the U-235 for use," according to outlawlabs.com, "along with the design of the warhead mechanism and the altitude at which it detonates, the explosive force of the A-bomb can range anywhere from 1 kiloton (which equals 1,000 tons of TNT) to 20 megatons (which equals 20 million tons of TNT - which, by the way, is the smallest strategic nuclear warhead we possess today. [Point in fact - One Trident Nuclear Submarine carries as much destructive power as 25 World War II's])."

While uranium is an ideally fissionable material, it is not the only one, plutonium can be used in an atomic bomb as well. By leaving U-238 inside an atomic reactor for an extended period of time, the U-238 picks up extra particles (neutrons especially) and gradually is transformed into the element plutonium.

"Plutonium is fissionable, but not as easily fissionable as uranium," continues outlawlabs.com. "While Uranium can be detonated by a simple 2-part gun-type device, Plutonium must be detonated by a more complex 32-part implosion chamber along with a stronger conventional explosive, a greater striking velocity and a simultaneous triggering mechanism for the conventional explosive packs. Along with all of these requirements comes the additional task of introducing a fine mixture of Beryllium and Polonium to this metal while all of these actions are occurring. Supercritical mass for Plutonium is defined as 35.2 lbs (16 kgs). This amount needed for a supercritical mass can be reduced to a smaller quantity of 22 lbs (10 kgs) by surrounding the Plutonium with a U-238 casing."

A plutonium bomb requires a lead shield. "The lead shield's only purpose is to prevent the inherent radioactivity of the bomb's payload from interfering with the other mechanisms of the bomb. The neutron flux of the bomb's payload is strong enough to short circuit the internal circuitry and cause an accidental or premature detonation.

"Fuses are implemented as another safeguard to prevent an accidental detonation of both the conventional explosives and the nuclear payload. These fuses are set near the surface of the nose of the bomb so that they can be installed easily when the bomb is ready to be launched. The fuses are installed only shortly before the bomb is launched. To affix them before it is time could result in an accident of catastrophic proportions."

There are two types of fission mechanics in terms of actually igniting the explosion : a gun method or an implosion method. With the gun method, "One mass of uranium is fired down a barrel into another mass of uranium. This is the simplest design and was used for the Hiroshima bomb," reported Ware. The most efficient method is the implosion method. The bomb that was detonated near Nagasaki was an implosion bomb. In the implosion methods, Ware's report continued, "A sphere of fissile material – plutonium or highly-enriched uranium – is surrounded by conventional high explosives, which are detonated simultaneously. Timing of the detonation is crucial for the material to be compressed sufficiently and uniformly."

A FUSION BOMB

"In fusion bombs, deuterium and tritium – two isotopes of hydrogen – are fused together to create heavier atoms," explained Ware. For fusion to take place, there must be very high pressure and a very high temperature. Basically, this is the kind of reaction that occurs on the sun. "In a nuclear weapon these are created through using a fission explosion (i.e. an atom bomb) to trigger the fusion reaction. There is no theoretical limit to the explosive force of a fusion weapon. Typically, fusion weapons are 10 to 100 times as explosive as the fission bombs which nearly destroyed Hiroshima and Nagasaki," Ware stated.

A DIRTY BOMB

In a dirty bomb, there is no splitting or fusing of any elements, nor is there any danger of such an event occurring, since critical mass cannot be achieved, even by accident. In such a dirty bomb, radioactive materials, in any quantity or of any grade, can be packaged with any amount of conventional explosive. "A dirty bomb is in no way similar to a nuclear weapon. The presumed purpose of its use would be therefore not as a Weapon of Mass Destruction but rather as a Weapon of Mass Disruption," reported the U.S. Nuclear Regulatory in a press release.

The detonation of a dirty bomb comes in two stages. The first stage is the blast. The blast is the detonation of the conventional explosion. It has two purposes. The first purpose is to destroy on impact, in the way TNT does. The second purpose of the blast is dispersal. The idea is that the blast incinerates the radioactive material, and, by virtue of the force of the blast, disperses radioactive particles in a targeted area.

The second stage of a dirty bomb is the radioactive material. It is not meant to be used in a truly nuclear capacity (i.e., splitting an atom), but because radioactive particles are in and of themselves dangerous to human life. As particles are dispersed, suddenly an entire area can be coated with a fine layer of radioactive powder that then begins to affect the inhabitants.

The effects of the radiation are not immediate and may go undetected for years. But long-term effects might be radiation sickness, high rates of cancer, high infant mortality, and sickness brought on by a compromised immune system.

"Depending on the sophistication of the bomb, wind conditions, and the speed with which the area of the attack was evacuated, the number of deaths and injuries from a dirty bomb explosion might not be substantially greater than from a conventional bomb explosion," reported the Cable News Network.

However, unlike its nuclear brethren a dirty bomb is relatively easy to create. Many plans can be obtained for building explosive devices. It wasn't that long ago that you could find bomb plans on the internet or in U.S. Army manuals. And procuring material for and building a nuclear weapon is far easier than anything a nuclear program could imagine.

"Radiological attacks constitute a credible threat. Radioactive materials that could be used for such attacks are stored in thousands of facilities around the U.S., many of which may not be adequately protected against theft by determined terrorists," Henry Kelly testified before the Senate Foreign Relations Committee on March 6, 2002, on the threat of radiological attack by terrorist groups. "Some of this material could be easily dispersed in urban areas by using conventional explosives or by other methods.

"While radiological attacks would result in some deaths, they would not result in the hundreds of thousands of fatalities that could be caused by a crude nuclear weapon. Attacks could contaminate large urban areas with radiation levels that exceed EPA health and toxic material guidelines," he continued.

"Materials that could easily be lost or stolen from U.S. research institutions and commercial sites could contaminate tens of city blocks at a level that would require prompt evacuation and create terror in large communities even if radiation casualties were low. Areas as large as tens of square miles could be contaminated at levels that exceed recommended civilian exposure limits. Since there are often no effective ways to decontaminate buildings that have been exposed at these levels, demolition may be the only practical solution. If such an event were to take place in a city like New York, it would result in losses of potentially trillions of dollars."

It is probably more accurate to describe dirty bombs, as Steven E. Koonin, provost at the California Institute of Technology, does, as weapons of "mass disruption" that could spread fear and disrupt daily life. "These weapons are not about terror. They are about psychological fear and they are about economic destruction, not casualties."

Richard Meserve, chairman of the Nuclear Regulatory Commission, said the health consequences from the use of a dirty bomb would be minimal and said the greater concern was a "psycho-social one."

The effects could also be more long-lasting than any other type of strike, said John Pike, director of the Global Security Organization. "You have long-term potential health hazards and you also have longer-term psychological social and political impacts that can go on weeks, months, maybe years," he said.

According to the U.S. Nuclear Regulatory Commission, "Basically, the principal type of dirty bomb, or Radiological Dispersal Device (RDD), combines a conventional explosive, such as dynamite, with radioactive material. In most instances, the conventional explosive itself would have more immediate lethality than the radioactive material. At the levels created by most probable sources, not enough radiation would be present in a dirty bomb to kill people or cause severe illness. For example, most radioactive material employed in hospitals for diagnosis or treatment of cancer is sufficiently benign that about 100,000 patients a day are released with this material in their bodies.

"However, certain other radioactive materials, dispersed in the air, could contaminate up to several city blocks, creating fear and possibly panic and requiring potentially costly cleanup. Prompt, accurate, non-emotional public information might prevent the panic sought by terrorists."

The commission also reports, "A second type of RDD might involve a powerful radioactive source hidden in a public place, such as a trash receptacle in a busy train or subway station, where people passing close to the source might get a significant dose of radiation."

CONCLUSION

While a dirty bomb in no way resembles the devastating power of an actual nuclear weapon, it would undoubtedly result in the loss of lives, many immediate casualties, and certainly long-range damaging effects that would have repercussions for years.

"Linkages have been made in devices that have been used in different continents...We know that we have the same bomb maker, or different bomb makers are using the same instructions."

– Unidentified Government Investigator

CHAPTER 4:

POSSIBLE TYPES OF BOMBS AND DELIVERY METHODS

A BOMB-MAKING NETWORK

As late as February 22, 2004, David Johnston quoted U.S. government investigators in the *New York Times* as saying they "found indications of a global bomb-making network, and have concluded that Islamic militant bomb builders have used the same designs for car bombs in Africa, the Middle East and Asia."

One government investigator said, "Linkages have been made in devices that have been used in different continents. . . . We know that we have the same bomb maker, or different bomb makers are using the same instructions."

"Experts. . .have begun to compile a data bank about bombs used by terrorists by examining tiny bits of housings, wirings, fuses, switches and the chemical composition of the explosives," reported worldnetdaily.com (an Internet newswire) in a story entitled "Bomb-making Network Exposed by U.S. Probe." "They've also investigated the electronic signatures of remote switching devices often used to detonate the devices." The piece went on to say, "In some cases, experts have been able to obtain evidence of who made the bomb through fingerprints or DNA material left behind, according to the report." The information was disseminated through the Terrorist Explosive Device Analytical Center (Tedac), a new forensic intelligence unit based at the FBI lab in Quantico, Virginia. Johansen reported that the FBI "had found that in the last five years almost 90 percent of terrorist attacks against Americans have involved improvised explosives."

"Tedac is a multiagency effort to analyze improvised explosive devices," said Dwight E. Adams, director of the FBI laboratory. "It gathers and shares intelligence related to the construction of these devices. Its purpose is to save lives."

While many intelligence officials believed that efforts to cripple Al Qaeda have largely succeeded, the reduced terrorist group still had the ability to communicate instructions around the world. With car bombs being detonated in places like New York City, Mumbai, Nairobi, Afghanistan, and Iraq, among other places, it was important to investigate these events. It has been conjectured that many of the key bomb makers learned to make improvised field munitions at Al Qaeda's training camps in the 1990s in Afghanistan, and that operatives are making sure the information is getting around.

This story confirms that governments around the world are concerned about just such events repeating, until global terrorism can be controlled, and that we are all at risk, whether we live in the U.S., Europe, the Middle East, Asia, the Subcontinent, or anywhere else. This is a world problem that will continue for some time before it finally abates.

TYPES OF BOMBS

One thing that makes the dirty bomb so attractive to terrorist organizations is that it can be packaged in a number of ways, and numerous combinations of materials can be used to make it. The other thing is size. A small dirty bomb no bigger than a shoe box can cause the same concern and panic that a larger bomb can, only it's easier to conceal.

Bomb makers over the years have used an ever-widening range of technologies to deliver bigger and bigger payloads. The three most dangerous and most easily bought would be TNT, dynamite, and ammonium nitrate (also known as a fertilizer bomb).

TNT

Certainly TNT is one of the most well known high explosives in the world. TNT (or trinitrotoluene as it is correctly known) "is a pale yellow crystalline, aromatic hydrocarbon compound that melts at 81°C," according to the U.S. Department of Health and Human Services. "Trinitrotoluene is an explosive chemical and a part of many explosive mixtures, such as when mixed with ammonium nitrate to form amatol.

"In its refined form, Trinitrotoluene is fairly stable, and unlike nitroglycerine, it is relatively insensitive to friction, blows or jarring. This means that it must be set off by a detonator. It does not react with metals or absorb water, and so is very stable for storage over long periods of time, unlike dynamite. But it is readily acted upon by alkalis to form unstable compounds that are very sensitive to heat and impact."

2,4,6-Trinitrotoluene has been known to enter the environment in wastewaters and solid wastes resulting from the manufacture of the compound, the processing and destruction of bombs and grenades, and the recycling of explosives. It moves in surface water and through soils to ground water. In surface water, it is rapidly broken down into other chemical compounds by sunlight. It is broken down more slowly by microorganisms in water and sediment. Small amounts of it can accumulate in fish and plants.

One might be exposed to 2,4,6-Trinitrotoluene by drinking contaminated water that has migrated from a chemical waste disposal site, or breathing contaminated air, or eating contaminated foods such as fruit and vegetables.

Workers involved in the production of explosives who were exposed to high concentrations of airborne 2,4,6-Trinitrotoluene in the workplace experienced several harmful health effects, including anemia and abnormal liver function. Similar blood and liver effects, as well as spleen enlargement and other harmful effects on the immune system, have been observed in animals that ate or breathed 2,4,6-trinitrotoluene in. Other effects in humans include skin irritation after prolonged skin contact, and cataract development after long-term exposure (365 days or longer).

DYNAMITE

Nitroglycerin was discovered in 1847 by Italian chemist Ascanio Sobrero. Nineteen years later, a Swedish scientist, Alfred Nobel, invented dynamite in 1866. The original explosive mixture being "75 percent nitroglycerin and 25 percent guhr (a porous, absorbent material that made the product easier to control and safer to use)," according the Encyclopaedia Britannica. "Nobel developed gelatinous dynamite in 1875 by creating a jelly from the dissolution of a collodion-type nitrocotton in nitroglycerin, producing a more powerful explosive than the straight dynamites and one that proved to be safer."

Dynamite is a high explosive used for blasting, consisting essentially of a mixture of, but not limited to, nitroglycerin, nitrocellulose, ammonium nitrate, sodium nitrate, and carbonaceous materials.

AMMONIUM NITRATE

Ammonium nitrate is used as a fertilizer and is supposed to be available from agricultural supply stores or perhaps well-stocked garden shops. It may be increasingly hard to find, however, due to its ease of use as an explosive, and especially since the Oklahoma City bombing. Ammonium nitrate is a combination of ammonium hydroxide and nitric acid. The bomb used by Timothy McVeigh was a combination of ammonium nitrate and diesel fuel, a particularly violent and potent mixture. And a very dangerous one, too, but very effective. This same lethal mixture's effects were also evident at the World Trade Center in 1993.

OTHER BOMBS OR EXPLOSIVE MATERIALS AND TERMS

Amatol: Amatol was developed by the British in World War I as a way of conserving their meager TNT supplies. It is composed of AN and TNT in varying ratios, the most common being 80:20. It is slightly more efficient than TNT when used in breaching charges, but since it contains AN it is somewhat hygroscopic and must be well sealed against moisture. It has a detonation velocity of 16,000 feet per second, almost twice that of straight AN. It is very insensitive, and while this makes it safe to handle (in fact, the blocks can be cut up with a hand saw), it can also makes it harder to detonate.

Ammonpulver: AP was developed in the late 1880s as a replacement for black powder. It is an intimate mixture of ammonium nitrate and charcoal. It was used by Germany and Austria as an artillery propellant until nitrocellulose-based powders became commonly available. It was extremely powerful, being on a par with double-based powders containing 30 percent nitroglycerine, and was virtually smokeless and flashless.

Unfortunately, AP had two drawbacks that made it undesirable as a propellant. First, since it was based on AN, it was extremely hygroscopic; second, when it was heated to moderate temperatures (32.10C), a change in the crystalline structure caused the powder grains to crumble, which drastically increased the chamber pressure of guns using this propellant, often causing burst muzzles.

However, this same instability is a virtue in bomb making, since AP is an excellent filler. It is very cheap to make - about thirty to forty cents a pound - and is quite insensitive to friction. But it is much harder to ignite than black powder. Filler preferred by terrorists for making pipe bombs or related items.

Ammonium tri-iodide: This chemical is very easy to obtain, and very easy to make. However, it is extremely dangerous to mix if not done so properly. A dangerous high explosive. Ammonium tri-iodide is so incredibly sensitive when it dries that it has been known to blow up at only the slightest touch.

ANFO: An explosive consisting of ammonium nitrate and fuel oil.

Animal blood bomb: A U.S. Army invention from the Improved Munitions Handbook (1969). A mixture of animal blood, gasoline, and other common household items, including Epsom salts and sugar among others. The animal blood acts as a gelling agent, giving this bomb's burning fuel the ability to adhere to target surfaces.

Astrolite: Astrolite is not a chemical compound but rather a two-component high-explosive mixture. Claims that it has the highest explosive velocity of any chemical explosives, a distant second only to a nuclear blast, are entirely false. The truth is, its low density makes it unlikely to achieve a detonation comparable to more common explosives Astrolite G is a mixture of ammonium nitrate and hydrazine; Astrolite A adds aluminum powder to the mix for extra power. Hydrazine is a highly toxic, corrosive, and dangerous chemical that is difficult to find at best. If breathed in a confined area, the fumes can kill you in seconds.

Battery: Made from a common battery that has been disassembled, processed, and then added to hydrogen peroxide.

Black powder: A deflagrating or low-explosive compound of an intimate mixture of sulfur, charcoal, and an alkali nitrate (usually potassium or sodium nitrate).

Blasting agent: Any material or mixture consisting of fuel and oxidizer intended for blasting, but not otherwise defined as an explosive, which means that the finished product, as mixed for use or shipment, cannot be detonated by means of a no. 8 blasting cap when unconfined.

Bulk mix: A mass of explosive material prepared for use in bulk form without packaging.

Commercial explosives: Explosives designed, produced, and used for commercial or industrial applications rather than military ones.

Common chemicals: Any element or chemical compound that, as part of a mixture, would be necessary for that mixture to be considered explosive; or any element or chemical compound that could be classified as an oxidizer or as a readily available fuel.

C-4 (Composition 4): A military plastic/moldable high-explosive. C-4 is the standard-issue plastic explosive used by the U.S. military. It retains its moldability over a broader range of temperatures, doesn't exude liquid (as Semtex does), and is pound for pound the most powerful explosive in common use today. Its power, stability, and versatility are un- equaled.

Custard powder bomb: Made with custard powder, rubber tubing, a tin, and a candle, this low grade flammable bomb can be used as a delayed trigger for a larger bomb.

Emulsions: A blend of water-in-oil emulsion and solid particulate inorganic oxidizing salt, mostly ammonium nitrate, also sodium nitrate will do he work.

Filler: A type of explosive/incendiary/chemical substance that, in combination with a fusing and/or firing system, constitutes an improvised explosive device (e.g., dynamite, match heads, gasoline).

Flammable liquid, combustible: Material that ignites easily and burns readily (i.e., gasoline, charcoal lighter fluid, diesel fuel, and paint thinners).

Fuel: Any substance that reacts with oxygen in the air or oxygen yielded by an oxidizer to facilitate combustion.

HMTD: Hexamethylene triperoxide diamine, an explosive.

Low explosives: Characterized by deflagration, a rapid combustion that moves through an explosive material at a velocity less than the speed of sound.

Nitrogen (N): One of the three primary nutrients for plants, along with phosphorus (P) and potassium (K).

Other: The category includes: match heads, military explosives (excluding C4 and TNT), improvised mixtures, flares, boosters, detonating cord, gases, blasting caps, PETN, RDX, HMTD, model rocket propellant, and smoke grenades.

Oxidizer or Oxidizing material: A substance, such as a nitrate, that readily yields oxygen or other oxidizing substances to stimulate the combustion of organic matter or other fuel.

PETN: An pentaerythritol tetranitrate explosive.

Photoflash and Fireworks powder: An explosive intended to produce an audible report and a flash of light when ignited; typically contains potassium perchlorate, sulfur or antimony sulfide, and aluminum metal.

RDX: Cyclonite, hexogen, T4, cyclo-1,3,5,-trimethylene-2,4,6-trinitramine; hexahydro-1,3,5,-trinitro S-triazine, an explosive.

Smokeless powder: Any of a class of explosive propellants that produce comparatively little smoke on explosion and consist mostly of gelatinized cellulose nitrates.

Specialty explosives: Any specialty tool used for a particular purpose other than blasting, such as explosive-actuated device (jet tappers, jet perforators), propellant-actuated power device (construction nail guns), commercial C-4, detasheet, oil well perforating guns, etc.

SLURRY: An explosive material containing substantial portions of a liquid, oxidizer, and fuel, plus a thickener.

TATP: Triacetone Triperoxide, a highly sensitive primary explosive manufactured from such common chemicals as acetone, peroxide, and acid.

TNT: Trinitrotoluene.

Urea ammonium nitrate (UAN): UAN solution is a popular liquid fertilizer in the United States and other industrialized countries.

Water gel: An explosive material containing substantial portions of water, oxidizers, and fuel, plus a cross-linking agent which may be a high explosive or blasting agent.

DELIVERY SYSTEMS

For as many types of bombs as there are, there are even more ways in which those bombs can be packaged or delivered. From something as big as a car, van, or truck, to something as small as a briefcase, knapsack, or duffel bag, each can pack an explosive, destructive blast capable of killing many civilians and injuring many more. The following delivery systems have been commonly used by terrorists and other extremists.

CARS, TRUCKS AND VANS

A car bomb is a device that is placed in a vehicle to be exploded while in the vehicle. Terrorists and assassins favor the car bomb because it acts as its own delivery mechanism and can involve a large amount of explosives without attracting suspicion. Truck bombs are also popular: trucks can crash through barriers more easily and can hold even more explosives. This ability to carry a bigger payload makes it a truly devastating dirty bomb, and has intelligence officials around the world the most worried. A truck bomb would be would be a device that could disperse a radioactive package over the widest possible area.

Terrorists typically employ one or more suicide bombers to ram a car into a building and simultaneously detonate it. With assassination, it is more common for the bomb to be affixed to the underside of the car and then detonated by remote control, by the car's motion, or by some other means. The bomb explodes as the target approaches or starts the vehicle, or more typically, once in motion so that the target is guaranteed to be inside. For this reason, bodyguards often check the underside of vehicles with a long mirror mounted on a pole.

Defending against a car bomb involves keeping cars away from buildings and reinforcing buildings to withstand an explosion. Forever burned into people's minds around the world are the vans used in the Oklahoma City and first World Trade Center attack. Certainly India, Israel, and several countries in Africa, and other countries throughout Asia, and the Pacific Rim have witnessed the destructive power of the car bomb.

There is no doubt that these types of bombs are lethal. Timothy McVeigh used fertilizer and diesel fuel to make the bomb that ripped through the Alfred P. Murrah Federal Building in Oklahoma City, Oklahoma, on April 19, 1995, at 9:02 a.m., killing 168 people, 19 of them children, and injuring hundreds of others.

Other infamous car bombings include the Mumbai blasts of 1993, masterminded by nefarious Indian mobster Dawood Ibrahim, which resulted in the deaths of 257 innocent pedestrians and workers; the 1998 bombing of the U.S. embassies in Kenya and Tanzania, killing 224 victims; and the bombing in Bali, Indonesia, whereon October 12, 2002, 202 people lost their lives.

Here's more:

A PARTIAL LIST OF CAR BOMBINGS

When	Where	Deaths	Type
February 11, 2004	Iraqi Army facility, Baghdad, Iraq	47	car bomb
February 10, 2004	Police station, Iskandariya, Iraq	53	truck bomb
January 31, 2004	Police station, Mosul, Iraq	9	car bomb
January 18, 2004	Coalition headquarters, Baghdad, Iraq	31	truck bomb
December 31, 2003	Restaurant, Baghdad, Iraq	8	car bomb
December 27, 2003	Coalition targets, Karbala, Iraq	19	car bombs (4)
December 25, 2003	Assassination attempt, Islamabad, Pakistan	14	truck bombs
December 14, 2003	Police station, Khaldiyah, Iraq	20	car bomb
November 22, 2003	Police stations, Iraq	18	car bombs (2)
November 20, 2003	British targets, Istanbul, Turkey	32	truck bombs
November 15, 2003	Two synagogues, Istanbul, Turkey	30	truck bombs
November 12, 2003	Italian military headquarters in Nasiriyah, Iraq	33	truck bomb
November 8, 2003	Riyadh, Saudi Arabia	18	truck bomb
October 27, 2003	Baghdad, Iraq	35	car bombs (4)
October 12, 2003	Baghdad Hotel, Baghdad, Iraq	6	car bomb
October 8, 2003	Police station, Baghdad, Iraq	9	car bomb
August 29, 2003	Mosque, Najaf, Iraq	85	car bomb
August 25, 2003	Mumbai, India	52	car bombs (2)

When	Where	Deaths	Type
August 19, 2003	United Nations headquarters, Baghdad, Iraq	22	truck bomb
August 7, 2003	Jordanian embassy, Baghdad, Iraq	19	truck bomb
August 5, 2003	Marriot Hotel, Jakarta, Indonesia	12	car bomb
August 1, 2003	Mozdok, Russia (near Chechnya)	50	truck bomb
May 12, 2003	Riyadh, Saudi Arabia	35	car bombs (4)
May 12, 2003	Znamenskoye, Chechnya	59	truck bomb
February 10, 2003	Bogota, Colombia	32	car bomb
December 27, 2002	Government buildings, Grozny, Chechnya	72	truck bombs
November 28, 2002	Hotel in Mombasa, Kenya	13	car bomb
October 21, 2002	Bus near Hadera, Israel	14	car bomb
October 12, 2002	Bali, Indonesia	202	car bomb
September 5, 2002	Kabul, Afghanistan	30	car bomb
June 14, 2002	U.S. consulate, Karachi, Pakistan	12	truck bomb
June 5, 2002	Bus, Megiddo Junction, Israel	17	car bomb
May 8, 2002	Bus, Karachi, Pakistan	14	car bomb
April 11, 2002	Synagogue, Djerba, Tunisia	21	truck bomb
April 7, 2002	Villavicencio, Colombia	12	car bomb
March 21, 2002	U.S. embassy, Lima, Peru	9	car bomb
October 1, 2001	Assembly building, Srinagar, Kashmir	38	car bomb
June 19, 2001	Gudermes, Chechnya	12	car bombs (3)
March 24, 2001	Mineralnye Vody, Russia	19	car bomb
March 5, 2001	BBC offices, London, Great Britain	0	car bomb
January 26, 2001	San Sebastian, Spain	1	car bomb
July 3, 2000	Grozny, Chechnya	25	truck bomb
September 4, 1999	Russian military apartment, Buinaksk, Dagestan	64	car bomb

When	Where	Deaths	Type
September 5, 1998	Apartment, Makhachkala, Dagestan	17	car bomb
August 15, 1998	Omagh, Northern Ireland	29	car bomb
August 7, 1998	U.S. embassies in Nairobi, Kenya, and Tanzania	224	car bombs (2)
March 5, 1998	Street, Colombo, Sri Lanka	36	mini-bus bomb
November 19, 1997	Hyderabad, India	23	car bomb
October 15, 1997	World Trade Center, Colombo, Sri Lanka	18	truck bomb
June 25, 1996	Khobar Towers, Dhahran, Saudi Arabia	19	truck bomb
January 31, 1996	Central Bank, Colombo, Sri Lanka	90	truck bomb
December 21, 1995	Market, Peshawar, Pakistan	45	car bomb
November 19, 1995	Egyptian embassy in Islamabad, Pakistan	15	truck bomb
November 13, 1995	U.S military headquarters in Riyadh, Saudi Arabia	7	car bomb
April 19, 1995	Federal building, Oklahoma City, United States	168	truck bomb
February 27, 1995	Zakho, Iraq	76	car bomb
January 30, 1995	Market, Algiers, Algeria	42	car bomb
July 18, 1994	Jewish center, Buenos Aires, Argentina	86	car bomb
April 6, 1994	Bus, Afula, Israel (First suicide bombing in Israel)	8	car bomb
June 21, 1993	Madrid, Spain	7	car bomb
May 27, 1993	Uffizi Gallery, Florence, Italy	6	car bomb
March 12, 1993	Mumbai, India (see 1993 Mumbai bombings)	257	car bombs
February 26, 1993	World Trade Center, New York City, USA	6	truck bomb
July 16, 1992	Shopping district, Lima, Peru	24	car bombs (2)
March 17, 1992	Israeli embassy, Buenos Aires, Argentina	29	car bomb
May 12, 1990	Bogota and Cali, Colombia	39	car bombs (3)

When	Where	Deaths	Type
May 16, 1989	Beirut, Lebanon	22	car bomb
April 14, 1988	USO club, Naples, Italy	5	car bomb
July 14, 1987	Karachi, Pakistan	72	car bombs (2)
July 5, 1987	Army camp, Jaffna, Sri Lanka	40	truck bomb
August 19, 1986	Public square, Tehran, Iran	20	car bomb
March 17, 1986	Military compound, Damascus, Syria	60	truck bomb
September 12, 1985	Checkpoint, South Lebanon	20	car bomb
August 17, 1985	Market, Beirut, Lebanon	55	car bomb
August 8, 1985	Rhein-Main Air Base, Frankfurt, West Germany	2	car bomb
May 22, 1985	Beirut, Lebanon	50	car bomb
March 10, 1985	Israeli convoy, Southern Lebanon	12	car bomb
March 8, 1985	Beirut, Lebanon	80	car bomb
September 20, 1984	U.S. embassy in Beirut, Lebanon	23	car bomb
December 21, 1983	French Army building, Beirut, Lebanon	15	truck bomb
December 12, 1983	U.S. and French embassies in Kuwait City, Kuwait	6	truck bombs
November 4, 1983	Israeli Army headquarters in Tyre, Lebanon	60	truck bomb
October 23, 1983	French Paratroop barracks in Beirut, Lebanon	58	truck bomb
October 23, 1983	U.S. Marines barracks in Beirut, Lebanon	241	truck bomb
May 20, 1983	Air Force Base in Pretoria, South Africa	20	car bomb
April 18, 1983	U.S. Embassy in Beirut, Lebanon	63	car bomb
February 2, 1983	Palestinian Research Center, Beirut, Lebanon	20	car bomb
January 28, 1983	PLO building, Beirut, Lebanon	45	car bomb
October 2, 1982	Central square, Tehran, Iran	60	truck bomb

When	Where	Deaths	Type
September 14, 1982	Phalangist office, Beirut, Lebanon	26	car bomb
May 24, 1982	French embassy, Beirut, Lebanon	14	car bomb
December 15, 1981	Iraqi embassy, Beirut, Lebanon	61	car bomb
October 1, 1981	PLO Office, Beirut, Lebanon	83	car bomb
May 17, 1974	Dublin and Monaghan, Northern Ireland	33	car bombs (2)
May 11, 1972	U.S. Army headquarters, Frankfurt, Germany	1	car bomb
March 30, 1965	U.S. embassy, Saigon, South Vietnam	20	car bomb
March 11, 1948	Jewish Agency in Jerusalem, Palestine	11	car bomb

ASSASSINATIONS BY CAR BOMBINGS (BY DATE)

When	Where	Target	Type
February 13, 2004	Doha, Qatar	Zelimkhan Yandarbiyev, Former, Chechen President	remote
November 20, 2003	Istanbul, Turkey	Roger Short, British consul general	suicide truck bomb
August 29, 2003	Najaf, Iraq	Ayatollah Mohammed Baqr al-Hakim, Iraqi cleric (with 84 others)	remote
August 19, 2003	Baghdad, Iraq	Sérgio Vieira de Mello, UN special representative (with 21 others)	suicide truck bomb
March 5, 2003	Paris, France	Rene Chalon	ignition-based
May 20, 2002	Beirut, Lebanon	Mohammed Jihad Ahmed Jibril, son of PFLP-GC leader Ahmed Jibril	unknown
January 24, 2002	Beirut, Lebanon	Elie Hobeika, Phalangist militia leader	remote
February 22, 2000	Vitoria, Spain	Fernando Buesa, Basque Socialist Party leader	remote
October 21, 1999	Ankara, Turkey	Ahmet Taner Kislali, prominent Turkish intellectual	tilt-based
July 30, 1990	London, England	Ian Gow, Conservative MP	dynamite
May 16, 1989	Beirut, Lebanon	Hassan Khaled, Lebanese spiritual leader (with 21 others)	remote
June 28, 1988	Athens, Greece	William Nordeen, U.S. military attache	remote
September 14, 1982	Beirut, Lebanon	Bashir Gemayel, Phalangist "president" (and 25 others)	timer
March 30, 1979	Palace of Westminster, Great Britain	Shadow Northern Ireland Secretary Airey Neave	tilt-based
September 21, 1976	Washington, D.C., U.S.	Orlando Letelier, Chilean exile	unknown
June 2, 1976	Phoenix, Arizona, U.S.	Don Bolles, investigative reporter	remote (dynamite)
September 30, 1974	Buenos Aires, Argentina	Carlos Prats, Former Chilean Army commander	car bomb
December 4, 1928	Chicago, U.S.	"Dapper" Danny Hogan, mobster	unknown

SUITCASES, LUGGAGE, AND BACKPACKS

As the incident on New Year's Eve 2003 clearly illustrated, U.S. and world intelligence officials are very worried about smaller packages detonated inside large crowds, or places where crowds gather. The World Series, the Super Bowl, World Cup events, major cricket, rugby and tennis matches – all attract large, international crowds, and all attract the media giving terrorists the biggest bang for the buck (so to speak).

"An explosive RDD – often called a dirty bomb – is any system that uses the explosive force of detonation to disperse radioactive material," claims a CIA report entitled "Terrorist CBRN: Materials and Effects." "A simple explosive RDD consisting of a lead-shielded container – commonly called a 'pig' – and a kilogram of explosive attached could easily fit into a backpack."

Officials are looking for people carrying backpacks, duffel bags and suitcases that are not large enough to attract attention and which can be taken to a place where an explosion can garner the largest body count quickly and easily, such as on a subway, a commuter train, bus, or at a shopping mall.

SUITCASE NUKES

The National Terror Alert Resource and Information Center (NTARC) reported, "A 'suitcase' bomb is a very compact and portable nuclear weapon and could have the dimensions of 60 x 40 x 20 centimeters or 24 x 16 x 8 inches. The smallest possible bomb-like object would be a single critical mass of plutonium (or U-233) at maximum density under normal conditions. The Pu-239 weighs 10.5 kg and is 10.1 cm across. It doesn't take much more than a single critical mass to cause significant explosions ranging from 10-20 tons. These types of weapons can also be as big as two footlockers. The warhead consists of a tube with two pieces of uranium, which, when rammed together, would cause a blast. Some sort of firing unit and a device that would need to be decoded to cause detonation may be included in the 'suitcase.'"

NTARC also reported that another highly portable weapon is a "backpack" bomb. The Soviet nuclear backpack system was developed in the 1960s for use in a time of war against NATO targets, and consists of three 'coffee can-sized' aluminum canisters in a bag. In order to explode, all three must be connected to make a single unit. The detonator is about 6 inches long. It has a 3-5 kiloton yield, depending on the efficiency of the explosion. It's kept powered during storage by a battery line connected to the canisters.

WHAT ARE THE EFFECTS OF A SUITCASE NUKE?

According to NTARC, radiation exposure occurs when either part of or all of the body is externally exposed to an outside source, such as standing near the site where a radiological device is set off, and either it can be absorbed by the body or can pass right through it.

Contamination occurs when radioactive materials in solid, liquid or gas form are released into the air and contaminate the body externally, internally, or both. For example, the skin might become contaminated, and/or the body might become contaminated, via the lungs, gut, or a wound.

Incorporation of radioactive material into the body occurs when cells, tissues, and such organs as the bone, liver, thyroid, or kidney are contaminated.

Gamma radiation can travel many meters in the air and many centimeters once inside the body; therefore representing a major external threat, and dense material is needed as a shield. Beta radiation can travel meters in air but can only moderately penetrate human skin, so clothing and some protection can help. Alpha radiation travels a very short distance through the air and can't penetrate the skin at all, but it can be harmful if inhaled, swallowed, or absorbed through an open wound.

Radiation exposure in the first hour following an explosion is about 90 percent, dropping off to about 1 percent after two days. It only drops to trace levels only after 300 hours.

HOW REAL IS THE THREAT OF A SUITCASE NUKE?

In September of 1997, on CBS's 60 Minutes, it was revealed that in the May of that same year, "Former Russian Security Council Secretary Aleksandr Lebed has stirred controversy in both Russia and the United States with his allegations that the Russian government is currently unable to account for some eighty small atomic demolition munitions (ADMs) which were manufactured in the USSR during the Cold War," as reported by Scott Roberts for the Center for Nonproliferation Studies. To the absolute horror of the entire international community, another high-ranking Russian official close to President Yeltsin confirmed the assertion as true not long after.

Conjecture surrounded the report for years. Had another nuclear power bought the suitcases? Worse yet, had a rogue government bought them? Or, even more horrifically, had they disappeared into Russia's infamous black market? No one knew.

And then, in December 2002, President Bush and British Prime Minister Tony Blair were both notified that Osama bin Laden had bought twenty suitcase nukes for cash from former KGB agents. Author Paul L. Williams released the story he had uncovered in a book entitled Al Qaeda: Brotherhood of Terror. "The deal is reportedly one of three in the last decade in which al-Qaida purchased small nuclear weapons or weapons-grade nuclear uranium," reported worlddailynet.com.

Williams claimed that bin Laden began his search in 1998, when he hired a team of five nuclear scientists from Turkmenistan. These were former employees at the atomic reactor in Iraq before it was destroyed by Israel. "The team's project was the development of a nuclear reactor that could be used 'to transform a very small amount of material that could be placed in a package smaller than a backpack.

"By 1990 bin Laden had hired hundreds of atomic scientists from the former Soviet Union for $2,000 a month – an amount far greater that their wages in the former Soviet republics," Williams continued. "They worked in a highly sophisticated and well-fortified laboratory in Kandahar, Afghanistan."

However, there is a lot of skepticism out there about the story. And rival stories have also appeared. "On February 8, 2004, a London-based Arab newspaper, *Al-Hayat*, reported that in 1998, in Kandahar, Afghanistan, al-Qaeda had bought nuclear weapons from Ukraine using the services of a Ukrainian scientist," reported Nikolai Sokov, in "'Suitcase Nukes': Permanently Lost Luggage," for the Center for Nonproliferation Studies. These allegations are not new. In 1998 another London-based Arab daily, *Al-Watan Al-Arabi*, reported that 20 'suitcase nukes' had been acquired by Chechen separatists.

Sokov sighted other sources saying that Ledbed's study was incomplete, since certain former Soviet agencies had not shared information with the task force he had assembled. But to this day, the infamous mystery of the many suitcase bombs remains unsolved.

IMPROVISED NUCLEAR DEVICE (IND)

"An IND is intended to cause a yield-producing nuclear explosion. An IND could consist of diverted nuclear weapon components, a modified nuclear weapon, or indigenous-designed device," according to the CIA's "Terrorist CBRN: Materials and Effects" report. "INDs can be categorized into two types: implosion and gun assembled. Unlike RDDs that can be made with almost any radioactive material, INDs require fissile material-highly enriched uranium or plutonium-to produce nuclear yield."

BOMB LAWS IN THE UNITED STATES

Congress made it illegal to sell, disseminate, or in any other way broadcast the information necessary to make a bomb. Mostly, it was successful. Many websites featuring these gruesome tidbits of knowledge were shut down, despite the best efforts of groups concerned with First Amendment issues. However, the information is still out there. Older, already published books are easy to find at any Army and Navy surplus store, in used-book shops, etc. There is enough information in these books to make a bomb. And, while the most infamous of these titles was and remains William Powell's legendary *The Anarchist's Cookbook and Homemade Weapons* (published in 1971), there are numerous Army manuals that have much the same information. Such pockets of information remain fairly easy to obtain, despite the best efforts of Congress to keep them out of circulation.

At the time of the writing of this book, we were able to obtain enough information from the web alone to make a bomb, including several out-of-date Army manuals and the supplies to do it.

CONCLUSION

The conclusion is simple. Al Qaeda, or some other terrorist group, would love nothing more than to strike yet another blow against the United States and America's allies. Bombs, whether they are in cars, backpacks, or even vests, are more and more common, not in Israel, but in Spain, in India, India, throughout Africa and Asia and indeed, around the world. The desire to hurt the U.S. and free world is very real, and the dirty bomb is a greater threat than ever before.

In February 2004, Joe Schelling, of the
Department of Energy's Sandia National
Laboratories told Newswise, a national media
outlet, in February of 2004, that he had recorded,
among hundreds, one story where "a small,
yttrium-90 sealed source was left
in a New York City cab."

CHAPTER 5:

CLOSER THAN YOU THINK

The threat of a dirty bomb is more real than people think. It is well known that Al Qaeda and other extremists want to set off a dirty bomb, and the parts are easy enough to find. It's the ease of finding these parts that has caused real worry to not just U.S. intelligence officials, but to the intelligence community around the world.

"Al-Qaida's apparent interest in acquiring nuclear technology came to the fore in 2001 when two Pakistani nuclear scientists were arrested after meeting Osama bin Laden in Afghanistan on suspicion of giving away secrets," reported the Associated Press on February 11, 2004, citing an interview with Cofer Black, the U.S. State Department's top antiterror expert. "The scientists were later released without being charged,"

"There are millions of radiation sources worldwide that terrorists could use to turn into dirty bombs - and controls to prevent them being stolen are poor in over a hundred countries," reported New Scientist, regarding a news release by the UN International Atomic Energy Agency (IAEA) in Vienna in June 2002.

"After September 11, we started looking at where terrorists might get the material for a dirty bomb," Jack Caravelli of the U.S. Department of Energy, who runs a uranium and plutonium security program told New Scientist. "Then we realized how many sources of radioactive material there are out there," he told *New Scientist*.

However, the idea of the dirty bomb has easily overshadowed the idea of detonating a nuclear blast, since it would be so much easier and cheaper to accomplish. One of the main reasons the dirty bomb has come to the fore is the ease with which the parts can be assembled. The conventional bomb part is already a part of the terrorist's repertoire; with only a little investigation finding the other highly radioactive parts is easier than one would like to image, both here and abroad.

FINDING RADIOACTIVE MATERIALS IN THE U.S.

"Significant amounts of radioactive materials are stored in laboratories, food irradiation plants, oil drilling facilities, medical centers, and many other sites," reported Henry Kelly, President Federation of American Scientists, who testified before the Senate Foreign Relations Committee on March 6, 2002. "Cobalt-60 and cesium-137 are used in food disinfection, medical equipment sterilization, and cancer treatments. During the 1960s and 1970s the federal government encouraged the use of plutonium in university facilities studying nuclear engineering and nuclear physics. Americium is used in smoke detectors and in devices that find oil sources."

Unfortunately, finding highly radioactive parts in the United States is just not that difficult. Take the 1997 story of the ten year-old New Jersey boy who took home an EXIT sign from a construction site. The sign had been carefully sealed to be safe, but the boy forced open the casing and released an amount of radiation equal to the radiation a human being is exposed to over a three-month period. The clean-up took more than two weeks, and the resulting bill, including an extended hospital stay for the boy totaled approximately $150,000 between state costs and personal fees incurred by the family. That should paint a fairly clear picture of how easy it is to create a dirty bomb.

There was another story filed in March 2001 in which a soil gauge was reported stolen from a Howard County, Maryland, construction site. "The gauge, used to measure how well the dirt is packed under roadways and pipelines, contains harmful radioactive material," reported Pierre Thomas for ABC News on April 12, 2002.

In February 2004, Joe Schelling, of the Department of Energy's Sandia National Laboratories, told Newswise, a national media outlet, that he had recorded among hundreds, one story where "a small, yttrium-90 sealed source was left in a New York City cab." Such claims, which once seemed innocuous – a teen prank, some joy riders – may have more ominous overtones today.

"More than 1,500 radioactive devices have been stolen, lost or abandoned since 1997, and the federal government can only account for 660 of those devices," reported Thomas. This account was followed by reports from licensed operators to the Nuclear Regulatory Commission. By then 835 of the missing devices were counted as lost.

The two stories quickly convey the importance of taking these issues very seriously. Across the country, food irradiation companies, hospitals and small clinics, construction companies, companies involved in heavy industry, power plants, laboratories, and a host of other unsuspecting businesses are now the stockyards for would be terrorists, many with large amounts of cobalt 60, strontium 90, or caesium 137.

BOY BUILDS NUCLEAR REACTOR

Maybe the simplest and even more disturbing demonstration of the ease and ingenuity with which one can go about building a dirty bomb is the 1995 story of David Hahn, of Clinton Township, Michigan. The tall, skinny young boy was the product of a divorced family, living during the week with his father and stepmother, spending weekends with his mother and stepfather.

David was a prodigy. By the age of twelve, he'd read with exacting scrutiny, a whole series of college-level chemistry text books by twelve years of age, and by the time he was fourteen he had made nitroglycerin. But David was more cunning and more ambitious than his persona and years would belie. The Boy Scout who had earned a Merit Badge in Atomic Energy, which had spurred his interest then, concocted a phony name and passed himself off as a high school physics instructor to get information and advice from the National Regulatory Commission. They were always willing to help teachers, and besides, no one was afraid anything could come of such information, since the NRC already knew of any substantial sales of radioactive materials - or so they thought.

David had uncovered enough information to build himself a "neutron gun." Basically, it was a minireactor. According to Ken Silverstein who recounted the amazing story in *Harper's* magazine, and who recently published a book about it, "David learned that a tiny amount of the radioactive isotope americium-241 could be found in smoke detectors. He contacted smoke-detector companies and claimed that he needed a large number for a school project. One company sold him about a hundred broken detectors for a dollar apiece." With his gun completed, after adding the lithium from a thousand lithium batteries, he fired it up. There in the shed in back of his mother's house, he attempted to make uranium 233. He failed. He had succeeded more than anyone could have possibly imagined, but fell just short of his goals.

He then decided to make a radium gun, finding plenty of old radium clocks in junkyards and antique shops around town. That too failed, but only just barely. By the end of this long and sordid story, David had in fact created a small breeder reactor, which not only generates electricity but also creates fissionable material. "Ignoring safety, David mixed his radium and americium with beryllium and aluminum, all of which he wrapped in aluminum foil, forming a makeshift reactor core," wrote Silverstein. "He surrounded this radioactive ball with a blanket of small foil-wrapped cubes of thorium ash and uranium powder, tenuously held together with duct tape."

On June 26, 1995, the seventeen year old finally gave himself up when his makeshift core started to really heat up, and began pouring out obscene amounts of radiation. The NRC came to town after the local police reported the situation.

This story once again illustrates the dangers inherent in feeling too safe. Whether the Office of Homeland Security can lock down enough stuff or not, the genie is already out of the bottle. Hundreds of everyday products contain radioactive parts, each in and of themselves not dangerous. But what is so absolutely dangerous about what David Hahn accomplished? If he had been an anarchist or even a terrorist, the product of his genius (despite awful marks in math and English in school), the first dirty bomb or suitcase nuke, might have completely dwarfed anything Al Qaeda has "accomplished" thus far.

While there have been books and even a movie about David's little experiment, it did put almost forty thousand people at risk, according to some EPA officials, and the cleanup cost $140,000. And for the educated terrorist bomb makers, it is easy enough to make an RDD without dying assembling it. David was an inventive seventeen year-old, but with all the materials available, especially in Russia and other nations, it is not unlikely that a top Al Qaeda bomb maker is on the project already.

And as for David Hahn? He now works for the Navy, a deckhand on the USS Enterprise.

ABDULLAH AL MUJAHIR (A.K.A. JOSE PADILLA)

On June 11, 2002, news shot across the world that Adullah Al Mujahir, an Al Qaeda operative, had attempted to slip into the United States. His mission? To do early prep work for a dirty bomb attack. The announcement had many very important aspects.

Attorney general John Ashcroft crowed, and for good reason. First, they had foiled a suspected dirty bomb plot. Second, it proved that Al Qaeda was interested in pursuing a dirty bomb scenario. Third, the arrest had come after a joint mission between the CIA and the FBI (who have not always played together nicely in the past), who used information provided by a former senior Al Qaeda figure,

Abu Zubaydah, who had been captured by U.S. authorities.

However, while the story was good for a few headlines, the truth behind the plot proved suspect. Abdullah was originally born Jose Padilla, in Brooklyn, New York, on October 18, 1970. He moved to Chicago five years later. A good kid gone bad, Padilla then went from a gang member to fanatical Muslim while in lockup.

Jose Padilla had been in and out of trouble his whole life, with a rap sheet that included aggravated battery, armed robbery, attempted armed robbery, as well as a 1991 arrest for firing a weapon in public at two men at a gas station. No one was hurt, but he did time and in 1998 another warrant was issued on an unrelated charge. Padilla fled and went abroad, spending most of his time in the Middle East. While there, he spent most of his time in Pakistan and Afghanistan, where he met with top Al Qaeda operatives.

According to Ashcroft, who made the dramatic announcement while traveling in Moscow, "While in Afghanistan and Pakistan, Al Muhajir trained with the enemy, including studying how to wire explosive devices and researching radiological dispersion devices."

"Officials suggest al Muhajir had approached Abu Zubaydah and other senior Al Qaeda leaders in Pakistan last December and suggested a dirty bomb attack in the U.S., reported *Time* magazine. "They liked the fact that al Muhajir had a U.S. passport, and trained him in wiring explosives, while he did research on the Internet into radiological dispersion."

After popping up on CIA/FBI radar due to a passport violation, Padilla was arrested, having travelled back and forth between Pakistan, Egypt, and Switzerland, when he flew into Chicago's O'Hare Airport on May 8, 2002.

It turned out that Jose Padilla's case was not as far along as the department might have liked, and he has since become a political hotcake with the government holding him on charges since his arrest, suspending the usual citizen's rights, citing his being an alleged enemy combatant. Civil liberties groups have taken Ashcroft's decision and department all the way to the Supreme Court, who agreed to hear the case.

While Padilla did enter the U.S. with $10,000 in his pocket and an agenda for scouting locations, further evidence shows that Al Qaeda may not have expected very much from this excited, but limited, volunteer.

With him sitting in federal prison awaiting his fate, his story illustrates that Al Qaeda is very serious about their intentions. As one official pointed out throughout the initial news coverage, Al Qaeda officials were more worried about finding a good operative than the technology of making a dirty bomb. It might speak to the fact that they are already there.

IT'S NOT JUST THE U.S.

With so many places in the United States making radioactive material so easily available, it's a wonder anyone would shop anywhere else. The problem is, there's even more available in Europe and the former Soviet Union. We're like a Seven-Eleven compared to their Walmart.

And dirty bomb targets aren't just inside U.S. borders. Indeed, Canada, the U.K., and others (as Madrid sadly and dramatically proved), especially Pakistan and India, have received alarming warnings that they might indeed be subjected to a demonstration of Al Qaeda's might.

On January 14, 2004, the Royal Canadian Mounted Police found themselves responding to worries in Ottawa. "Up to 40 RCMP cruisers patrolling the capital will be fitted with dirty bomb detectors amid rising fears of a terrorist strike involving radiological weapons," Jim Bronskill reported for the Canadian Press.

"Officials are particularly concerned about a so-called dirty bomb packed with conventional explosives such as dynamite to scatter radioactive material."

"Significant radiological resources could be acquired by terrorists," stated a RCMP release, "through clandestine theft or low-level military operations and moved, possibly undetected, to urban population areas or to targets of high symbolic value,".

"There are also some 30,000 old sources stored in Europe "at risk of being lost from regulatory control," reported the *New Scientist*, regarding a news release by the UN International Atomic Energy Agency (IAEA) in Vienna in June of 2002, "and up to 70 going missing every year. Worldwide, the IAEA has confirmed reports of 263 smuggling attempts involving radiation sources since 1993."

The problem is even surfacing in Greece, home of the 2004 Summer Olympics.

On January 14, 2004, it was reported that, according to NNSA Administrator Linton Brooks, the National Nuclear Security Administration and Greece were installing radiation detectors at seven locations around the country. "After Greece asked the International Atomic Energy Agency for help in heading off a potential dirty bomb attack, the U.N. agency in turn requested U.S. assistance with the project," reported Global Security Newswire. "Besides installing detectors, NNSA is giving the IAEA $500,000 for equipment to be used at Olympic venues."

However, the three most dangerous countries remain the former Soviet Republics, Pakistan, and India. The ultimate radioactive shopping jag is easily the former Soviet Republics. Jon Ronson, a writer for the Manchester Guardian, wrote an exceptional piece on dirty bombs for his newspaper in August 2002. The Guardian charged him with building some kind of nuclear device, and cheaply. He began his search for the perfect radioactive piece with an expert at the Nuclear Threat Initiative, a think tank in Washington, D.C.

"One does not want to provide a cookbook for terrorists," Matthew Brunn, a top special at the think tank quipped. Still, the expert indicated Russia.

"If I was building a dirty bomb, that's what I would do. In the nuclear age, they were building nuclear airplanes and nuclear rocketships," Brunn told Ronson. "They were digging canals using nuclear bombs. There was a great deal of nuclear enthusiasm, and now loads of these big, hulking, nasty radioactive sources are scattered around all over."

Indeed, the web and other media outlet are choked with scads of interesting stories to substantiate his claim. Brunn passed along the well-known story of the four lumberjacks in Lja who around Christmas time, 2001, found this thing somewhere deep in the frozen Georgian woods, with all the snow around it melted. It was warm all right, so the hefty men brought it back to camp with them to keep them warm. Unfortunately for them, it was a discarded part of a thermonuclear generator. All the men ended up spending months in intensive care. Stories like these are not uncommon.

"Radiothermal generators are quite common in Georgia, on

the Black Sea," reported Joby Warrick for the *Washington Post*. "In the far-eastern Russian region of Chukotka, investigators discovered a complete breakdown in controls over 85 radiothermal generators placed along the arctic coast by the Soviets in the 1960s and '70s. Some of the machines had been vandalized for scrap metal, others were literally falling into the surf and at least one could not be found."

But the generators story was not Warrick's biggest. A year and a half later it was missile warheads. It turned out that the former Soviet Union had outfitted thirty-eight Alazan surface-to-surface missiles (with a range of about 10 miles) with dirty bomb warheads. More important, those warheads were now missing. According to intelligence sources, they allegedly could be found in the remote country Transdniester Moldovan Republic. In this small country (smaller than Rhode Island), black market arms dealers enjoy an incredible haven from the outside world, which is all the more reason security officials around the world are concerned.

"For terrorists, this is the best market you could imagine: cheap, efficient, and forgotten by the whole world," Vladimir Orlov, founding director of the Center for Policy Studies in Moscow, told Warrick. Even with more than fifty thousand tons of artillery shells and other murderous equipment for sale, the warheads were especially troubling.

In April 2002, Defense Secretary William Cohen told a Senate panel that the best place to find the parts for a dirty bomb was Russia. Senator Joseph Biden agreed. "There are many sources for weapons of mass destruction. But there is one place that has it all. That place is Russia." Biden pointed out that Russia possessed approximately 1,000 metric tons of highly enriched uranium and

160 metric tons of weapons-grade plutonium.

Since these announcements, officials from the U.N., the United States, and Russia have pledged to secure many of the parts and materials that seem to have seemingly been forgotten since the demised of the Soviet state. And, there have been addition but unsubstantiated reports that Al Qaeda has been duped several time by savvy con men and ruthless mafiosos who have swindled bin Laden out of millions with the promise of radioactive payloads that turned out to be hoaxes. Still, in a country where resources are scarce and money even more so, how efficient can we be in the face of an enemy as ruthless as Al Qaeda and a source as resourceful as the black market.

Maybe not so surprisingly, the most recent dirty bomb warnings targeted India and Pakistan. Pakistan's nuclear weapons program has been notoriously shady, allegedly selling nuclear secrets to other countries, including North Korea, Iran, and elsewhere. It has even been alleged that their success is tied to notorious Indian mobster and car bomb killer Dawood Ibrahim.

Michael Krepon, founder of the Henry L. Stinson think tank, told a U.S. Senate Committee that Pakistan and India were "very vulnerable" to the dirty bomb threat as reported in the Times of India on January 29, 2004. "Material that could be used to make 'dirty bombs' resides in many poorly guarded hospitals and civilian research labs in India and Pakistan."

PAKISTAN

There is no way to tell this huge story without including the recently reported news that Abdul Qadeer Khan, Pakistani nuclear scientist and father of his country's nuclear arsenal, allegedly sold nuclear secrets on the black market to many other countries. According to MSNBC, "Buhary Syed Abu Tahir, the alleged chief financier of an international nuclear trafficking network run by Khan, told Malaysian police that the scientist asked him to send two containers of used centrifuge parts from Pakistan to Iran in 1994 and 1995." The report also substantiated the claim that Libya and North Korea were also participants in the network, and bought secrets and materials from Tahir and Khan.

BORDER WORRIES

The U.S.-Canadian border is our largest, and, as was recently cited in several newspapers, it is largely unguarded. Vast stretches slice right through some of the most beautiful, rugged terrain found in all of North America. It is known worldwide that Al Qaeda considers this border an opportune place to cross into the United States with a dirty bomb.

In October 2003, Bill Gertz of the *Washington Times* reported that the FBI and CIA were searching for Adnan El Shukrijumah. The FBI claimed that he had been identified in March 2002 in Hamilton, Ontario, where he had been posing as a student at McMaster University, which has its own 5-megawatt research reactor, trying to obtain radioactive material.

"El Shukrijumah's connection to the dirty-bomb plot," reported Gertz, "is based on his stay in southern Florida at the same time as another al Qaeda suspect, Jose Padilla.

Al Qaeda pursued a 'dirty bomb.'"

"We have received a lot of good information from these detainees over the past several weeks," said William H. Parrish, a U.S. intelligence official, "and corroborated the fact there were active plans, ongoing, to conduct another attack in the United States.

This attack, as they indicated, was probably going to be multiple attacks – simultaneous."

NUCLEAR POWER PLANTS HERE AND ABROAD

Since 9/11, the Office of Homeland Security has increased security in and around nuclear power plants. However, some material discarded by those plants in years past has been lost. It's out there across the country in the wilderness or in scrap yards, sitting there, exuding lethal amounts of radiation, without anyone's knowing about it.

What could even be more devastating, however, is the idea of an airliner crashing into a nuclear power plant. In November 2001, the International Atomic Energy Agency (IAEA), according to the *New Scientist*, said, "The world's 1,300 nuclear facilities are not hardened to withstand 'acts of war' like a deliberate hit by a large, fully-fuelled passenger jet."

"There is no sanctuary anymore, no safety zone," warned Mohamed El Baradei, the IAEA's director general. Indeed, the *New Scientist* has been accused of "scaremongering" by British Nuclear Fuels, for reporting on an October 2001 threat to a power plant at Sheffield. That same month, *New Scientist* noted, based on FBI reports, "the air space around all U.S. nuclear plants was closed to private planes by the Federal Aviation Authority. The U.S. Nuclear Regulatory Commission also issued a 'threat advisory.'"

"The sheer psychological impact

is enormous. . . .

Many more people will be killed

from the stampede that follows

than from the bomb."

—Nikolai Sokov

CHAPTER 6:

THE EFFECTS OF A DIRTY BOMB ATTACK

Casualties, panic, and cost. These are the three major considerations of any RDD or dirty bomb, and are the essential ingredients that make it such a perfect weapon of aggression. Various studies, some done right after September 11, 2002, others as recently as January 2004, have discussed the effects of such an attack.

All agree that the weapon is less a "Weapon of Mass Destruction" and more a "Weapon of Mass Disruption." The casualties might range from scores of people to hundreds. The panic would be horrific. And the overall cost would extend beyond cleanup, bills, perhaps precipitating a massive downturn in many Western economies.

What is clear, however, is that with each passing year, the overarching feeling is that the more time we have to study it, the news gets worse.

CASUALTIES

"It is possible to kill a fair number of people and sicken a lot more, such that you begin to stress the healthcare system," wrote Peter D. Zimmerman. According to the *Washington Post*'s Joby Warrick, "The researchers derived estimates of human casualties from extensive studies of radiation accidents, including one in 1987 in Goiania, Brazil. In that case, workers ruptured a capsule of radioactive cesium . . . 249 people suffered from serious radiation injuries and four died."

The story of Goiania, Brazil, has often been quoted ever since the dirty bomb first came to people's attention. In 1985, a small privately owned clinic in the small city was closed by doctors when they moved to new offices. They left behind some old equipment. In 1987, their abandoned radiology machine was hacked apart by scavengers. Days later, a scrap yard worker broke open a cesium 137 casing, exposing glowing blue powder. Enamored with it, he showed the powder to his friends. Only three and a half ounces leaked from the casing, but thousands of people ended up being exposed to the radiation and sixty people were hospitalized.

On March 6, 2002, Henry Kelly, president of the Federation of American Scientists, testified before the Senate Foreign Relations Committee. In his remarks, he stated, "While radiological attacks would result in some deaths, they would not result in the hundreds of thousands of fatalities that could be caused by a crude nuclear weapon. Attacks could contaminate large urban areas with radiation levels that exceed EPA health and toxic material guidelines."

Mr. Kelly said that the effects would vary based on several different factors. First, the amount of radioactive material, and its density in terms of radioactive isotopes would come into play. He also cited wind speed and direction, placement of the bomb, size of the particles released, etc. Given these variables, he could project only a certain number of scenarios.

If it were a calm day, and the explosion emitted a fine mist, the victims "will be exposed to material in the dust inhaled during the initial passage of the radiation cloud, if they have not been able to escape the area before the dust cloud arrives. We assume that about twenty percent of the material is in particles small enough to be inhaled. If this material is an alpha emitter, it will stay in the body and lead to long term exposure." He also said that longtime residents would have to move, and that traffic, whether vehicle or pedestrian, would also carry alpha emitters ever farther afield, and lead to inhalation by still others.

While few would see deaths from the actual explosion, the real long-term effects would be radiation sickness and deaths from cancer. We know this from what we know about long-term exposure to radiation and inhalation of radioactive particles.

PANIC

In January 2004, UPI reporter T. K. Malloy quoted a research paper submitted to Air Command and Staff College at Maxwell Air Force Base, Alabama, by Majors Scott M. Michelson and Darren D. Medlin. "Panic would occur, just the words 'nuclear' or 'radiological' provokes fear in the U.S. public. At the first report of a radiological incident, the public will likely try to execute an uncontrolled evacuation from the area. . . . Panic might produce casualties and damage far in excess of the actual device itself."

In April 2002, Nikolai Sokov, an analyst at the Monterey Institute's Center for Non-Proliferation Studies, told Paul Richter of the Los Angeles Times, "The sheer psychological impact is enormous. . . . Many people will be killed from the stampede that follows than from the bomb."

On March 6, 2002, Richard Meserve, chairman of the Nuclear Regulatory Commission, told ABC News that the greater concern was a "psycho-social one . . . The terrorist's greatest weapon is fear."

And John Pike, director of the Global Security Organization, told ABC, "You have long-term potential health hazards and you also have longer-term psychological social and political impacts that can go on weeks, months, maybe years."

"The main purpose of a dirty bomb is to frighten people," stated a report from Idaho State University. "Most people in the public have no or little understanding of what radiation is or what the risks are from it. Due to this lack of knowledge and the likely media attention given to a dirty bomb, people will over react, to the extent of having more harm done by the reaction to the event than to the event itself."

Steven E. Koonin, provost at the California Institute of Technology, also chimed in in much the same way: "We are talking about a weapon of mass disruption more than destruction. These weapons are not about terror. They are about psychological fear and they are about economic destruction, not casualties."

COST

On January 13, 2004, when the Center for Technology and National Security Policy at the National Defense University released a report of a year-long study funded by the Pentagon that reexamined the effects of a dirty bomb incident on New York City or Washington, D.C., the news was startling and unmistakable. While few people would actually die from the explosion, or "mass casualties," the long-term effects would be ruinous, far more devastating economically and environmentally than the September 11 bombing of the World Trade Center.

"The threat of radiological attack on the United States is real, and terrorists have a broad palette of [radiological] isotopes to choose from. . . . It could cause tens to hundreds of fatalities under the right circumstances, and is essentially certain to cause great panic and enormous economic loses."

According to nuclear physicists Peter D. Zimmerman and Cheryl Loeb, a successful RD attack was likely to "equal and perhaps even exceed that of the September 2001 attacks. . . . The estimated cost to return the lower Manhattan to a condition prior to the September terrorist attacks was in excess of $30 billion. The immediate costs exceeded $11 billion." Cleanup costs might be greater with a dirty bomb, given that finely ground radioactive particles might be more difficult to eradicate than fallen debris from a building. Scenarios from other studies have ranged from a few city blocks up to ten. Demolishing and carting away ten block's worth of real estate to places unknown for burial underground or safe storage would be more time-consuming, and a much hotter political potato. No facility in the United States could handle that much radioactive debris. And what state would volunteer to do it?

Zimmerman and Loeb pointed out that while much of the World Trade Center recovery was covered by insurance companies, who were hard hit, "That would not be the case following an RDD attack, because radiation is a specifically excluded risk in virtually all policies written in the United States. The government will have to step in to subsidize economic recovery."

A small dirty bomb could pack anywhere from 1,000 to

10,000 curies (a curie is a unit measurement of radioactivity), Zimmerman and Loeb concluded, and could contaminate an area the size of the Mall in Washington, D.C. The cleanup would force the evacuation of thousands and take years.

Zimmerman and Loeb's report was shocking because many of the early reports saw the dirty bomb mainly as a scare weapon because of its nuclear connection more than its destructive prowess. Now the message is clear: A dirty bomb, if released in a New York City or Washington, D.C., would be very expensive, and its grotesque effects would have consequences for years to come.

If there is an explosion:

- Exit the building ASAP.
- Take shelter against your desk or a sturdy table.
- Do not use elevators.
- Check for fire and other hazards.
- Take your emergency supply kit if time allows.

If there is a fire:

- Exit the building ASAP.
- Crawl low if there is smoke
- Use a wet cloth, if possible, to cover your nose and mouth.
- Use the back of your hand to feel the upper, lower, and middle parts of closed doors.
- If the door is not hot, brace yourself against it and open slowly.
- If the door is hot, do not open it. Look for another way out.
- Do not use elevators.
- If you catch fire, do not run. Stop-drop-and-roll to put out the fire.
- If you are at home, go to a previously designated meeting place.
- Account for your family members and carefully supervise small children.
- Never go back into a burning building.

If you are trapped in debris:

- If possible, use a flashlight to signal your location to rescuers.
- Avoid unnecessary movement so that you don't kick up dust.
- Cover your nose and mouth with anything you have on hand. (Dense-weave cotton material can act as a good filter. Try to breathe through the material.)
- Tap on a pipe or wall so that rescuers can hear where you are.
- If possible, use a whistle to signal rescuers.
- Shout only as a last resort. Shouting can cause a person to inhale dangerous amounts of dust.

CHAPTER 7:

WHAT TO DO IN CASE
OF A DIRTY BOMB

The Office of Homeland Security established the National Terror Alert Resource Center (NTARC), whose *Terrorism Survival Guide* covers all possible dirty bomb scenarios, including biological, chemical, and nuclear. Passages are included here. Should you wish a more complete look, download the files at www.nationalterroralert.com. This book is exceptionally well thought out and thorough for those who feel the need for a more comprehensive survival plan in the face of continuing terrorist threats.

Because it is so dangerously difficult to obtain high-level radioactive materials from a nuclear facility, most materials used in a dirty bomb would come from a low-level radioactive source. Low-level sources are found in hospitals, on construction sites, and at food irradiation plants; they are used to diagnose and treat illnesses and sterilize instruments and equipment, to inspect welding seams, and to kill harmful microbes in food.

DANGERS OF A DIRTY BOMB

Because of its low-level radioactivity, the dirty bomb's primary danger would be the blast itself. Gauging actual radiation is difficult since the source is unknown. However, at the levels achieved by most dirty bombs, there is not enough radiation present to cause severe illness due to exposure.

What should people do following a dirty bomb explosion? Radiation cannot be seen, smelled, felt, or tasted by humans, so there is no way of knowing if radioactive materials were involved in the explosion. According to NTARC, if people are not too severely injured by the initial blast, they should:

Leave the immediate area on foot. Do not panic. Do not take public or private transportation such as buses, subways, or cars because if radioactive materials were involved, they may contaminate cars or the public transportation system.

Go inside the nearest building. Staying inside will reduce people's exposure to any radioactive material from a dirty bomb that may be on dust at the scene.

Remove clothes as soon as possible, place them in a plastic bag, and seal it. Removing clothing will remove most of the contamination caused by external exposure to radioactive materials. Saving the contaminated clothing will allow testing for exposure without invasive sampling.

Take a shower or wash as best you can. Washing will reduce the amount of radioactive contamination on the body and will effectively reduce total exposure.

Be on the lookout for information. Once emergency personnel can assess the scene and the damage, they will be able to tell people whether radiation was involved.

Even if people do not know whether radioactive materials were present, following these simple steps can help reduce their injury from other chemicals that might have been present in the blast.

IF RADIOACTIVE MATERIALS WERE INVOLVED

Keep televisions or radios tuned to local news networks. If a radioactive material was released, people will be told where to report for radiation monitoring and blood testing to determine whether they were exposed to the radiation, as well as what steps to take to protect their health.

TAKING POTASSIUM IODIDE (KI)

Potassium iodide protects only the thyroid gland from exposure to radioactive iodine. KI does not protect a person from other radioactive materials, or protect other parts of the body from radiation exposure. It must be taken prior to exposure (for example, hearing that a radioactive cloud is drifting your way) or immediately after to be effective. Since there is no way of knowing if radioactive iodine was used in a given device, taking KI would not be advised because it can be dangerous for some people.

RISK OF CANCER FROM A DIRTY BOMB

While some cancers are caused by exposure to radiation, being at the site of a dirty bomb explosion does not guarantee exposure to radiation. Only doctors using sensitive radiation detection devices are able to check people's skin to determine whether they were exposed. Being near a radioactive source for a short time, or being exposed to a small amount of radioactive material, does not mean a person will get cancer. A doctor can assess the risk once the level of exposure has been determined.

WHAT TYPES OF TERRORIST EVENTS MIGHT INVOLVE RADIATION?

Possibilities include introducing radioactive material into food or water supplies, using explosives like dynamite to scatter radioactive materials (a dirty bomb), bombing or destroying a nuclear facility, or exploding a small nuclear device.

Although contaminating food or water would cause great concern and even fear, the level of contamination would not be that high or increase the danger of adverse health effects.

Although a dirty bomb could cause serious injuries from the explosion, most likely it would not have enough radioactive material to cause serious radiation sickness among large numbers of people. However, depending on the dose, those directly exposed to radiation scattered by the bomb could have a greater risk of developing cancer later in life.

A meltdown or explosion at a nuclear facility could cause a large amount of radioactive material to be released. People at the facility would probably be contaminated and possibly injured if there was an explosion. Those receiving a large dose might develop acute radiation syndrome. People in the surrounding area also could be exposed or contaminated.

Clearly, exploding a nuclear device could result in a lot of property damage. People would be killed or injured or contaminated. Many would present symptoms of acute radiation syndrome. After such an explosion, radioactive fallout would extend over a large area far from the point of detonation, potentially increasing people's risk of developing cancer over time.

HOW CAN I PROTECT MYSELF DURING A RADIATION EMERGENCY?

After a release of radioactive materials, local authorities will monitor the levels of radiation and determine what protective actions to take.

The most appropriate action will depend on the situation. Tune to the local emergency response network or news station for information and instructions during any emergency.

If a radiation emergency involves the release of large amounts of radioactive materials, you may be advised to "shelter in place," which means to stay in your home or office; or you may be advised to move to another location.

If you are advised to shelter in place, you should do the following:
- Close and lock all doors and windows.
- Turn off fans, air conditioners, and forced-air heating units that bring in fresh air from the outside. Only use units to recirculate air that is already in the building.
- Close fireplace dampers.
- If possible, bring pets inside.
- Move to an sealed room or basement.
- Keep your radio tuned to the emergency response network or local news to find out what else you need to do.
- If you are advised to evacuate, follow the directions that your local officials provide. Leave the area as quickly and orderly as possible.

- Take your "Go Pack."
- Take pets only if you are using your own vehicle and going to a place you know will accept animals. Emergency vehicles and shelters usually will not accept animals.

WHAT IS RADIATION?

Radiation is a form of energy that is present all around us. There are different types of radiation, some of which have more energy than others. Amounts of radiation released into the environment are measured in units called "curies." However, the dose of radiation that a person receives is measured in "rem" units. For more information about radiation, check www.epa.gov/radiation or www.orau.gov/reacts/define.htm.

HOW CAN EXPOSURE OCCUR?

People are exposed to small amounts of radiation every day, from both naturally occurring sources (such as elements in the soil or rays from the sun) and man-made ones. Man-made sources include some electronic equipment (such as microwave ovens and television sets), medical sources (such as X-ray machines, certain diagnostic testing equipment, and treatment procedures), and from nuclear weapons testing.

The amount of radiation from either source is usually small; a radiation emergency (such as a power plant or terrorist event) could expose people to small or large doses of radiation, depending on the situation.

Scientists estimate that the average person in the United States receives a dose of about one-third of a rem per year. About 80 percent of human exposure comes from natural sources and 20 percent from man-made, mainly X rays.

"Internal exposure" refers to radioactive material being taken into the body through breathing, eating, or drinking.

"External exposure" refers to an exposure to a radioactive source outside the body.

"Contamination" refers to radioactive particles that are deposited anywhere that they are not supposed to be, such as on skin.

HEALTH EFFECTS OF RADIATION EXPOSURE

Radiation affects the body in different ways, but the adverse health effects may not be seen for many years. These effects range from mild, such as skin reddening, to serious, such as cancer and death. The severity of these effects is determined by the amount of radiation (the dose) absorbed by the body, the type of radiation, the means of exposure, and the duration of exposure.

Acute radiation syndrome (ARS), or radiation sickness, is usually caused when a person receives a high dose of radiation to the whole body in a matter of minutes. Survivors of Hiroshima and Nagasaki and firefighters responding to the Chernobyl disaster in 1986 experienced ARS. The immediate symptoms of ARS are nausea, vomiting, and diarrhea; later, bone marrow depletion may lead to weight loss, loss of appetite, feeling like you have the flu, infection, and bleeding. The survival rate depends on the radiation dose. For those who do survive, full recovery takes from a few weeks up to two years.

Children exposed to radiation may be more at risk than adults. Radiation exposure to the unborn child is of special concern because the human embryo and fetus are extremely sensitive to radiation.

And then there's the fact that radiation exposure, like exposure to the sun, is cumulative.

PROTECTING AGAINST RADIATION EXPOSURE

The three basic ways to reduce radiation exposure are:

Time. Decrease the amount of time you spend near the source of radiation.

Distance. Increase your distance from a radiation source.

Shielding. Increase the shielding between you and the radiation source. Shielding is anything that creates a barrier between people and the radiation source. Depending on the type of radiation, the shielding can range from something as thin as a plate of window glass or as thick as several feet of concrete. Being inside a building or a vehicle can provide shielding from some kinds of radiation

POTASSIUM IODIDE (KI) INFORMATION

Recent terrorist events have many people concerned about the potential for future attacks using radioactive materials. Taking potassium iodide (KI) tablets after such an incident may limit the risk to a person's thyroid gland from ionizing radiation exposure. The Centers for Disease Control and Prevention (CDC) prepared the following fact sheet to further explain when KI might be appropriate and what people should consider before making a decision to take it.

WHEN TO TAKE KI

Local emergency management officials will tell people when to take KI. If a nuclear incident occurs, officials will have to find out which radioactive substances are present before recommending that people take KI. If radioactive iodine is not present, then taking KI will not protect people. If radioactive iodine is present, then taking KI will help protect a person's thyroid gland from the radioactive iodine. Taking KI will not protect people from other radioactive substances that may be present along with the radioactive iodine.

The Food and Drug Administration (FDA) recommends that KI be taken as soon as the radioactive cloud containing iodine from the explosion is close by. KI may still have some protective effect even if it is taken 3 to 4 hours after exposure to radioactive iodine. Because the radioactive iodine will be present in the initial blast and decays quickly, a single dose of KI may be all that is required. The FDA recommendations on KI can be reviewed on the Web at www.fda.gov/cder/guidance/4825fnl.htm.

FORMS OF KI, AND HOW MUCH SHOULD BE TAKEN

KI comes in tablets of 130 mg. A one-time dose at the levels recommended in this fact sheet is usually all that is required. However, if a person expects to be exposed to radioactive iodine for more than 24 hours, another dose should be taken every 24 hours. People should listen to emergency management officials for recommendations after an incident. According to the FDA:

- Adults should take one 130 mg tablet.
- Children between 3 and 18 years of age should take one-half of a 130 mg tablet (65 mg).
- Children between 1 month and 3 years of age should take one-fourth of a 130 mg tablet (32 mg).
- Infants from birth to 1 month of age should be given one-eighth of a 130 mg tablet (16 mg).
- Women who are breastfeeding should take the adult dose, and their

infants should receive the recommended infant dose.

- Children who are approaching adult size (greater than or equal to 150 pounds) should take the adult dose regardless of their age.
- KI tablets can be stored for at least 5 years without losing their potency.

People should remember that taking a higher dose of KI, or taking KI more often than recommended, will not offer more protection and can cause severe illness and death due to allergic reaction.

HOW A NUCLEAR INCIDENT MIGHT CAUSE THYROID DAMAGE

Some types of radioactive incidents release radioactive iodine. The thyroid gland, which will use any iodine that is in a person's bloodstream, cannot tell the difference between radioactive and nonradioactive forms of iodine. Because of this, the thyroid would rapidly absorb radioactive iodine just as it does iodine from a person's diet. The radioactive iodine releases energy (radiation) that, in high concentrations, can damage the cells of the thyroid gland. In some people, especially young children, this damage can cause thyroid cancer or other diseases of the thyroid within a few years of the exposure.

WHAT IS KI?

KI is a salt of iodine. It is one of several ingredients that can be added to table salt to make it iodized. KI has also been approved by the FDA as a nonprescription drug for use as a "blocking agent" to prevent the human thyroid gland from absorbing radioactive iodine. However, KI may not provide people with 100 percent protection against all radioactive iodine. Its effectiveness will depend on a variety of factors, including when a person takes it, how much iodine is already in the person's thyroid, how fast the person's body processes it, and the amount of radioactive iodine the person is exposed to. Iodized table salt will not provide enough iodine to protect the thyroid and should not be used as a substitute.

WHY KI WOULD BE IMPORTANT IN THE EVENT OF A NUCLEAR INCIDENT

Because the thyroid will rapidly absorb any iodine that is in the body, people may need to take KI tablets soon after an incident that involves radioactive iodine. The KI will saturate the thyroid gland with iodine and help prevent it from absorbing radioactive iodine. However, KI does not prevent the effects of other radioactive elements. Using KI will only protect the thyroid gland from radioactive iodine. It will not protect other parts of the body from radioactive iodine, and it will not protect a person from other radioactive materials that may be released.

WHO SHOULD OR SHOULD NOT TAKE KI WHEN THE PUBLIC IS TOLD TO DO SO

Children are the most susceptible to the dangerous effects of radioactive iodine. The FDA and the World Health Organization (WHO) recommend that children from newborn to 18 years of age all take KI unless they have a known allergy to iodine.

Women who are breastfeeding should also take KI, according to the FDA and WHO, to protect both themselves and their breast milk. However, breastfeeding infants should still be given the recommended dosage of KI to protect them from any radioactive iodine that they may breathe in or drink in breast milk.

Young adults between the ages of 18 and 40 have a smaller

chance of developing thyroid cancer or thyroid disease from exposure to radioactive iodine than do children. However, the FDA and WHO still recommend that people ages 18 to 40 take the recommended dose of KI. This includes pregnant and breast-feeding women, who should take the same dose as other young adults.

Adults over the age of 40 have the smallest chance of developing thyroid cancer or thyroid disease after an exposure to radioactive iodine, but they have a greater chance of having an allergic reaction to the high dose of iodine in KI. Because of this, they are not recommended to take KI unless a very large dose of radioactive iodine is expected. People should listen to emergency management officials for recommendations after an incident.

MEDICAL CONDITIONS THAT MAKE IT DANGEROUS TO TAKE KI

The high concentration of iodine in KI can be harmful to some people. People should not take KI if they:

- Have ever had thyroid disease (such as hyperthyroidism, thyroid nodules, or goiter).
- Know they are allergic to iodine (as in x-ray dye or shellfish).
- Have certain skin disorders (such as dermatitis herpetiformis or urticaria vasculitis).
- Should consult their doctor if they are unsure whether to take KI.

FACTS ABOUT THE THYROID GLAND

The thyroid is a small gland located in a person's neck on either side of the breathing tube (trachea). The thyroid has two parts, a right lobe and a left lobe, that are connected by a small strip of tissue called the isthmus. The main function of the thyroid gland is to create, store, and release thyroid hormones. These hormones regulate the body's metabolism.

It is important to get iodine to the thyroid gland. The thyroid gland takes iodine from the bloodstream and uses it to make thyroid hormones. Without the required amounts of iodine, the thyroid will not be able to make these hormones. Most of the iodine in people's bodies comes from the food they eat.

PREPARING FOR A TERRORIST EVENT

Devastating acts, such as the terrorist attacks on the World Trade Center and the Pentagon, have left many concerned about the possibility of future incidents in the United States and their potential impact. They have raised uncertainty about what might happen next, increasing stress levels. Nevertheless, there are things you can do to prepare for the unexpected and reduce the stress that you may feel now and later should another emergency arise. Taking preparatory action can reassure you and your children that you can exert a measure of control even in the face of such events.

WHAT YOU CAN DO TO PREPARE

Finding out what can happen is the first step. Once you have determined the events possible and their potential in your community, it is important that you discuss them with your family or household. Develop a disaster plan together.

1. Create an emergency communications plan. Choose an out-of-town contact your family or household will call or e-mail to check on each other should a disaster occur. Your selected contact should live far enough away that they would be unlikely to be directly affected by the same event, and they should know they are the chosen contact. Make sure every household member has that contact's, and each other's, e-mail addresses and telephone numbers (home, work, pager and cell). Leave these contact numbers at your children's schools, if you have children, and at your workplace. Your family should know that if telephones are not working, they need to be patient and try again later or try e-mail. Many people flood the telephone lines when emergencies happen but e-mail can sometimes get through when calls don't.

2. Establish a meeting place. Having a predetermined meeting place away from your home will save time and minimize confusion should your home be affected or the area evacuated. You may even want to make arrangements to stay with a family member or friend in case of an emergency. Be sure to include any pets in these plans, since pets are not permitted in shelters and some hotels will not accept them.

3. Assemble a disaster supplies kit. If you need to evacuate your home or are asked to "shelter in place," having some essential supplies on hand will make you and your family more comfortable. Prepare a disaster supplies kit in an easy-to-carry container such as a duffel bag or small plastic trash can. Include "special needs" items for any member of your household (infant formula or items for people with disabilities or older people), first aid supplies (including prescription medications), a change of clothing for each household member, a sleeping bag or bedroll for each, a battery-powered radio or television and extra batteries, food, bottled water, and tools. It is also a good idea to include some cash and copies of important family documents (birth certificates, passports, and licenses) in your kit.

Copies of essential documents—powers of attorney, birth and marriage certificates, insurance policies, life insurance beneficiary designations, and a copy of your will—should also be kept in a safe location outside your home. A safe-deposit box or the home of a friend or family member who lives out of town is a good choice.

For more complete instructions, ask your local Red Cross chapter for the brochure *Your Family Disaster Supplies Kit.*

4. Check on the school emergency plan of any school-age children you may have. You need to know if they will they keep children at school until a parent or designated adult can pick them up or send them home on their own. Be sure that the school has updated information about how to reach parents and responsible caregivers to arrange for pickup. And, ask what type of authorization the school may require to release a child to someone you designate, if you are not able to pick up your child. During times of emergency the school telephones may be overwhelmed with calls.

For more information on putting together a disaster plan, request a copy of the brochure *Your Family Disaster Plan* from your local American Red Cross chapter. You may also want to request a copy of *Before Disaster Strikes…How to Make Sure You're Financially Prepared* for specific information on what you can do now to protect your assets.

IF DISASTER STRIKES

- Remain calm and be patient.
- Follow the advice of local emergency officials.

- Listen to your radio or television for news and instructions.
- If the disaster occurs near you, check for injuries. Give first aid and get help for seriously injured people.
- If the disaster occurs near your home while you are there, check for damage using a flashlight. Do not light matches or candles or turn on electrical switches. Check for fires, fire hazards, and other household hazards. Sniff for gas leaks, starting at the water heater. If you smell gas or suspect a leak, turn off the main gas valve, open windows, and get everyone outside quickly.
- Shut off any other damaged utilities.
- Confine or secure your pets.
- Call your family contact—do not use the telephone again unless it is a life-threatening emergency.
- Check on your neighbors, especially those who are elderly or disabled.

A WORD ON WHAT COULD HAPPEN

As we learned from the events of September 11, 2001, the following things can happen after a terrorist attack:

- There can be significant numbers of casualties and/or damage to buildings and the infrastructure. So employers need up-to-date information about any medical needs you may have and on how to contact your designated beneficiaries.
- Heavy law enforcement involvement at local, state, and federal levels follows a terrorist attack due to the event's criminal nature.
- Health and mental health resources in the affected communities can be strained to their limits, maybe even overwhelmed.
- Extensive media coverage, strong public fear, and international

implications and consequences can continue for a prolonged period.

- Workplaces and schools may be closed, and there may be restrictions on domestic and international travel.
- You and your family or household may have to evacuate an area, avoiding roads blocked for your safety.
- Cleanup may take many months.

EVACUATION

If local authorities ask you to leave your home, they have a good reason for making this request, and you should heed the advice immediately. Listen to your radio or television and follow the instructions of local emergency officials and keep these simple tips in mind:

- Wear long-sleeved shirts, long pants, and sturdy shoes so you can be protected as much as possible.
- Take your disaster supplies kit.
- Take your pets with you; do not leave them behind. Because pets are not permitted in public shelters, follow your plan to go to a relative's or friend's home, or find a "pet-friendly" hotel.
- Lock your home.
- Use travel routes specified by local authorities—don't use shortcuts because certain areas may be impassable or dangerous.
- Stay away from downed power lines.
- Listen to local authorities.
- Your local authorities will provide you with the most accurate information specific to an event in your area. Staying tuned to local radio and television, and following their instructions is your safest choice.

If you're sure you have time:

- Call your family contact to tell them where you are going and when you expect to arrive.
- Shut off water and electricity before leaving, if instructed to do so. Leave natural gas service on unless local officials advise you otherwise. You may need gas for heating and cooking, and only a professional can restore gas service in your home once it's been turned off. In a disaster situation it could take weeks for a professional to respond.

SHELTER IN PLACE

If you are advised by local officials to "shelter in place," what they mean is for you to remain inside your home or office and protect yourself there. Close and lock all windows and exterior doors. Turn off all fans, heating and air-conditioning systems. Close the fireplace damper. Get your disaster supplies kit, and make sure the radio is working. Go to an interior room without windows that's above ground level. In the case of a chemical threat, an above-ground location is preferable because some chemicals are heavier than air and may seep into basements even if the windows are closed. Using duct tape, seal all cracks around the door and any vents into the room. Keep listening to your radio or television until you are told all is safe or you are told to evacuate. Local officials may call for evacuation in specific areas at greatest risk in your community.

ADDITIONAL POSITIVE STEPS YOU CAN TAKE

Raw, unedited footage of terrorism events and people's reaction to them can be very upsetting, especially to children. We do not recommend that children watch television news reports about such events, especially if the reports show repeated images over and over again of the incident. Young children do not realize that it is repeated video footage and they think the event is happening again and again. Adults may also need to give themselves a break from watching disturbing footage. However, listening to local radio and television reports will provide you with the most accurate information from responsible governmental authorities on what's happening and what actions you will need to take. So you may want to make some arrangements to take turns listening to the news with other adult members of your household.

Another useful preparation includes learning some basic first aid. To enroll in a first aid and AED/CPR course, contact your local American Red Cross chapter. In an emergency situation, you need to tend to your own well-being first and then consider first aid for others immediately around you, including possibly assisting injured people to evacuate a building if necessary.

People who may have come into contact with a biological or chemical agent may need to go through a decontamination procedure and receive medical attention. Listen to the advice of local officials on the radio or television to determine what steps you will need to take to protect yourself and your family. As emergency services will likely be overwhelmed, only call 911 about life-threatening emergencies.

NUCLEAR AND RADIOLOGICAL ATTACK

Nuclear explosions can cause deadly effects—blinding light, intense heat (thermal radiation), initial nuclear radiation, blast, fires started by the heat pulse, and secondary fires caused by the destruction. They also produce radioactive particles called "fallout" that can be carried by wind for hundreds of miles.

Terrorist use of a radiological dispersion device (RDD) – often called a "dirty nuke" or a "dirty bomb" – is considered far more likely than use of a nuclear device. These radiological weapons are a combination of conventional explosives and radioactive material designed to scatter dangerous and sublethal amounts of radioactive material over a general area. Such weapons appeal to terrorists because they require very little technical knowledge to build and deploy compared to that of a nuclear device. Also, their radioactive materials, used widely in medicine, agriculture, industry, and research, are much more readily available and easy to obtain compared to weapons-grade uranium or plutonium.

Terrorist use of a nuclear device would probably be limited to a single smaller "suitcase" weapon. The strength of such a weapon can be seen in the range of the bombs used during World War II. The nature of the effect would be the same as a weapon delivered by an intercontinental missile, but the area affected and severity of the effect would be significantly more limited.

There is no way of knowing how much warning time there would be before an attack by a terrorist using a nuclear or radiological weapon. A surprise attack remains a possibility.

The danger of a massive strategic nuclear attack on the United States involving many weapons receded with the end of the Cold War. However, some terrorists have been supported by nations that have nuclear weapons programs.

If there were threat of an attack from a hostile nation, people living near potential targets could be advised to evacuate, or they could decide on their own to evacuate to an area not considered a likely target. Protection from radioactive fallout would require taking shelter underground, or in the middle of a large building.

In general, potential targets include:

- Strategic missile sites and military bases.
- Centers of government such as Washington, D.C., and state capitals.
- Important transportation and communication centers.
- Manufacturing, industrial, technology, and financial centers.
- Petroleum refineries, electrical power plants, and chemical plants.
- Major ports and airfields.

Taking shelter during a nuclear attack is absolutely necessary. There are two kinds of shelters: **blast** and **fallout**.

Blast shelters offer some protection against blast pressure, initial radiation, heat and fire, but even a blast shelter could not withstand a direct hit from a nuclear detonation.

Fallout shelters do not need to be specially constructed for that purpose. They can be any protected space, provided that the walls and roof are thick and dense enough to absorb the radiation given off by radioactive particles. The three protective factors of a fallout shelter are shielding, distance, and time.

Shielding. The more heavy, dense materials—thick walls, concrete, bricks, books, and earth—between you and the fallout particles, the better.

Distance. The more distance between you and the fallout particles, the better. An underground area, such as a home or office building basement, offers more protection than a first floor. A floor near the middle of a high-rise may be better, provided nothing is nearby where significant accumulations of fallout particles could collect. A flat roof collects particles, so the top floor is not a good choice; nor is a floor adjacent to a neighboring roof.

Time. Fallout radiation loses its intensity fairly rapidly. In time, you will be able to leave the fallout shelter. Radioactive fallout poses the greatest threat to people during the first two weeks, by which time it has declined to about 1 percent of its initial radiation level.

Remember that any protection, however temporary, is better than none at all, and the more shielding, distance, and time you can take advantage of the better.

ELECTROMAGNETIC PULSE

In addition to other effects, a nuclear weapon detonated in or above the earth's atmosphere can create an electromagnetic pulse (EMP), a high-density electrical field. EMP acts like a stroke of lightning but is stronger, faster, and briefer. EMP can seriously damage electronic devices connected to power sources or antennas. This include communication systems, computers, electrical appliances, and automobile or aircraft ignition systems. The damage could range from a minor interruption to actual burnout of components. Most electronic equipment within a thousand miles of a high-altitude nuclear detonation could be affected. Battery powered radios with short antennas generally would not be affected.

Although EMP is unlikely to harm most people, it could harm those with pacemakers or other implanted electronic devices.

WHAT TO DO BEFORE A NUCLEAR OR RADIOLOGICAL ATTACK

- Learn the warning signals and all sources of warning used in your community.
- Make sure you know what the signals are, what they mean, how they will be used, and what you should do if you hear them.
- Assemble and maintain a disaster supply kit with food, water, medications, fuel and personal items adequate for up to two weeks—the more the better.
- Find out what public buildings in your community may have been designated as fallout shelters. It may have been years ago, but start there, and learn which buildings are still in use and could be designated as shelters again.
- Call your local emergency management office.
- Look for yellow-and-black fallout shelter signs on public buildings. *Note: With the end of the Cold War, many of the signs have been removed from the buildings previously designated as shelters.*
- If no noticeable or official designations have been made, make your own list of potential shelters near your home, workplace, and school: basements, the windowless center area of a middle floor in a high-rise building, subways and tunnels.
- Give your household clear instructions about where fallout shelters are located and what actions to take in case of attack.
- If you live in an apartment building or high-rise, talk to the manager about the safest place in the building for sheltering, and about providing for building occupants until it is safe to go out.
- There are few public shelters in many suburban and rural areas. If you are considering building a fallout shelter at home, keep the following in mind.

- A basement, or any underground area, is the best place to shelter from fallout. Often, few major changes are needed, especially if the structure has two or more stories and its basement—or one corner of it—is below ground.
- Fallout shelters can be used for storage during nonemergency periods, but only store things there that can be very quickly removed. (When they are removed, dense, heavy items may be used to add to the shielding.)
- All the items you will need for your stay need not be stocked inside the shelter itself but can be stored elsewhere, as long as you can move them quickly to the shelter.
- Learn about your community's evacuation plans. Such plans may include evacuation routes, relocation sites, how the public will be notified, and transportation options for people who do not own cars and those who have special needs.
- Acquire other emergency preparedness booklets that you may need.

WHAT TO DO DURING A NUCLEAR OR RADIOLOGICAL ATTACK

- Do not look at the flash or fireball – it can blind you.
- If you hear an attack warning: Take cover as quickly as you can, below ground if possible, and stay there unless instructed to do otherwise.
- If you are caught outside, and are unable to get inside immediately, take cover behind anything that might offer protection. Lie flat on the ground and cover your head.
- If the explosion is some distance away, it could take 30 seconds or more for the blast wave to hit.
- Protect yourself from radioactive fallout. If you are close enough to see the brilliant flash of a nuclear explosion, the fallout will

arrive in about 20 minutes. Take shelter, even if you are many miles from ground zero – radioactive fallout can be carried by the winds for hundreds of miles. Remember the three protective factors: shielding, distance, and time.

- Keep a battery-powered radio with you and listen for official information. Follow the instructions given. Local instructions should always take precedence: officials on the ground know the local situation best.

WHAT TO DO AFTER A NUCLEAR OR RADIOLOGICAL ATTACK

In a public or home shelter:

- Do not leave the shelter until officials say it is safe. Follow their instructions when leaving.
- If you are in a fallout shelter, stay there until local authorities tell you it is permissible to leave. The length of your stay can range from a day or two to four weeks.
- Contamination from a radiological dispersion device could affect a wide area, depending on the amount of conventional explosives used, the quantity of radioactive material, and atmospheric conditions.
- A suitcase terrorist nuclear device detonated at or near ground level would produce heavy fallout from the dirt and debris sucked up into the mushroom cloud.
- A missile-delivered nuclear weapon would probably cause an explosion many times more powerful than a suitcase bomb and provide a greater cloud of radioactive fallout.
- The decay rate of the radioactive fallout would be the same, making it necessary for those in the areas with highest radiation levels to remain in shelter for up to a month.

- The heaviest fallout would be limited to the area at or downwind from the explosion, and 80 percent of the fallout would occur during the first twenty-four hours.
- Because of these facts and the very limited number of weapons terrorists could detonate, most of the country would not be affected by fallout.
- People in most of the areas that would be affected could be allowed to come out of shelter and, if necessary, evacuate to unaffected areas within a few days.
- Although it may be difficult, make every effort to maintain sanitary conditions in your shelter.
- Water and food may be scarce. Use them prudently, but do not impose severe rationing, especially for children, the ill, or the elderly.
- Cooperate with shelter managers. Living with many people in confined space can be difficult and unpleasant.

RETURNING TO YOUR HOME

Keep listening to the radio for news about what to do, where to go, and where not to go. If your home was within the range of a bomb's shock wave, or you live in a high-rise or other apartment building that experienced a non-nuclear explosion, check first for any sign of collapse or damage, such as:

- Toppling chimneys, falling bricks, collapsing walls, plaster falling from ceilings.
- Fallen light fixtures, pictures, and mirrors.
- Broken glass from windows.
- Overturned bookcases, wall units, or other fixtures.
- Fires from broken chimneys.

- Ruptured gas and electric lines.
- Immediately clean up spilled medicines, drugs, flammable liquids, and other potentially hazardous materials.
- Listen to your battery-powered radio for instructions and information about community services.
- Monitor the radio and television for information on assistance that may be provided. Local, state, and federal governments and other organizations will help meet emergency needs and help you recover from damage and losses.

The danger may be aggravated by broken water mains and fallen power lines.

If you turned gas, water, and electricity off at the main valves and switch before you went to shelter:

- Do not turn the gas back on. The gas company will turn it back on for you or you will receive other instructions.
- Turn the water back on at the main valve only after you know the water system is working and water is not contaminated.
- Turn electricity back on at the main switch only after you know the wiring is undamaged in your home and the community electrical system is functioning.
- Check to see that sewage lines are intact before using sanitary facilities.
- Stay away from damaged areas.
- Stay away from areas marked **radiation hazard** or **HAZMAT**.

"What is needed is cradle-to-grave control

of powerful radioactive sources to protect them

against terrorism or theft."

— Mohamed ElBaradei.

CHAPTER 8:

HOW TO PREVENT A DIRTY BOMB

Trying to prevent the detonation of a dirty bomb somewhere in the world is almost singularly impossible. However, there are steps that can be taken to reduce the chances of a RDD being unleashed on an unsuspecting civilian population, especially in a highly populated urban center.

Numerous government agencies have coordinated their efforts since September 11, 2001. International intelligence agencies have also been more cooperative and helpful regarding each other's ongoing investigations. As well, many national and international governments and other bodies have issued studies, reports, and convened panels to try to increase awareness and understanding of the issues surrounding a dirty bomb scenario.

"We have created a range of prevention programs that simply didn't exist before September 11, and refocused many that did," Robert S. Mueller, III, FBI Director told the Annual Conference of the American Muslim Council in Alexandria, Virginia, on June 28, 2002. "With nearly half a billion dollars in funds from Congress, we are overhauling our technology as quickly as we can given how far behind current capabilities we are today. To vastly improve our ability to manage and analyze information, we are hiring a crop of new analysts, borrowing resources from agencies like the CIA, and improving the skills of those on board. And we are rethinking and rebuilding relationships with a range of organizations and agencies, including our 650,000 colleagues in law enforcement nationwide."

Most agree that a three-pronged counterattack is the best solution. The first step is to continue to hobble and defeat Al Qaeda and other terrorist groups. This is the most difficult and complicated step. As long as the economies of many of the Arab states continue to falter, large populations of disaffected youth growing up in politically confusing times will go down the wrong path, choosing murderous means to justify their misguided ends. Numerous young men and women in Palestine, in fact, willingly volunteered for suicide missions. And there are always those in power who willingly sent them to their deaths.

Second, governments need to make the millions of small bits and pieces of radioactive materials more secure so they don't fall into the wrong hands. Easier said than done, but, again, by making the general population more aware of these issues, they can learn to keep a wary eye out for suspicious persons and events.

And third, we need to improve our response capabilities, and draw up realistic and better responses to such events. New York, Ottawa, London, Paris, Rome, Washington, D.C., Bombay (Mumbai), and many other cities around the world need to have better-equipped local law enforcement (i.e., dirty bomb detectors) and better medical response teams ready to take up the fight, and better-informed citizens who will not panic and heighten or multiply the sense of emergency in times of crisis. Easier said than done.

STEPS TO CUT OFF AL QAEDA AND OTHER TERRORIST ORGANIZATIONS

Obviously, in the last two and a half years, this has been the single biggest issue driving the Bush Administration. There have been great successes and incredible failures, but there is no doubt that Al Qaeda has been crippled by the efforts of the U.S. Army in Afghanistan and Iraq, and by the efforts of the FBI and CIA here at home as well as abroad.

On February 11, 2003, Robert S. Mueller, III, the Federal Bureau of Investigation's director, spoke before the Senate Select Committee on Intelligence on the War on Terrorism. The object of his fight is clear: "There can be no compromise or negotiated settlement. Accordingly, the prevention of another terrorist attack remains the FBI's top priority as we strive to disrupt and destroy terrorism on our soil."

In his statement, the FBI director pointed out the more than 197 arrests in 17 months, with 99 of those people being convicted at the time of that hearing. "Moreover, our efforts have damaged terrorist networks and disrupted terrorist plots across the country," the director stated. He highlighted the following:

- In Portland, Oregon, six were charged with providing material support to terrorists.
- In Buffalo, the FBI arrested seven Al Qaeda associates and sympathizers indicted in September 2002 for providing material support to terrorism.

- In Seattle, Earnest James Ujaama (a.k.a. Bilal Ahmed) was charged with conspiracy to provide material support to terrorists and suspected of establishing a terrorist training facility in Bly, Oregon.
- In Detroit, four were charged with document fraud and providing material support to terrorists.
- In Chicago, Benevolence International Foundation director Enaam Arnaout was charged with funneling money to Al Qaeda.
- In Florida, three US citizens were arrested for acquiring weapons and explosives in a plot to blow up an Islamic Center in Pinellas County in retaliation for Palestinian bombings in Israel.

Mueller also went on to point out how the FBI was successfully disrupting the sources of terrorist financing, including freezing $113 million from sixty-two organizations and conducting seventy investigations, twenty-three of which resulted in convictions. FBI investigations also made it more difficult for suspicious NGOs to raise money and continue operations. He also pointed out that donors began thinking twice about where they sent their money—some questioning the integrity of the organization they might be supporting and others fearful of being linked to an organization that may be under FBI scrutiny.

According to Mueller, the financial disruption operations also included an international dimension. For example, the FBI was instrumental in providing information that resulted in the apprehension of a major money launderer for Al Qaeda and the Taliban. Since the arrest, the subject's hawala network had been disrupted and dismantled in the UAE and in Pakistan, in part due to the efforts of the FBI.

SECURING EXISTING RADIOACTIVE AND NUCLEAR PARTS AND OPERATIONS

"What is needed is cradle-to-grave control of powerful radioactive sources to protect them against terrorism or theft," says IAEA director General Mohamed ElBaradei, reported *New Scientist* regarding a news release by the UN International Atomic Energy Agency (IAEA) in Vienna in June 2002.

On March 6, 2002, Henry Kelly, president of the Federation of American Scientists, testified before the Senate Foreign Relations Committee on the threat of radiological attack by terrorist groups. In his testimony, he outlined the major steps that have since been actively approached.

He requested that Congress, "Fully fund material recovery and storage programs. Hundreds of plutonium, americium, and other radioactive sources are stored in dangerously large quantities in university laboratories and other facilities. In all too many cases they are not used frequently, resulting in the risk that attention to their security will diminish over time." He also pointed out that disposal of these materials was difficult, since only the Department of Energy (DOE) was authorized to take possession and transport them to permanent disposal sites. He noted that even by that date, the DOE Off-Site Source Recovery Project had successfully secured over three thousand sources and had moved them to safe locations. He also pointed out that this program was underfunded and should be strengthen immediately.

Kelly also insisted that licensing, inspection procedures, and security requirements for all dangerous amounts of radioactive material be reviewed. Human Health Services, the DOE, the Nuclear Regulatory Commission, and other affected agencies should again be better funded and be given clear outlines how they too could fight the war of prevention. "A thorough reevaluation of security regulations should be conducted to ensure that protective measures apply to amounts of radioactive material that pose a homeland security threat, not just those that present a threat of accidental exposure."

Kelly also said that funding should go toward research aimed at finding alternatives to radioactive materials. "A research program aimed at developing inexpensive substitutes for radioactive materials in functions such as food sterilization, smoke detection, and oil well logging should be created."

Laxity is the main worry. Many wonder, as we get further and further away from September 11, 2001, that stringency will wane, as will our ardor. It must be impressed upon many individuals that Al Qaeda failed in 1993 to bring down the World Trade Center, and waited for the holes to open up again in our very open society. They tried again eight years later and succeeded. We cannot let our guard down at the federal, state, or local level, nor can the companies who control such dangerous materials become negligent or sloppy in their duties, for they have a very important trust placed in them by the government and its citizens.

IMPROVING RESPONSE SCENARIOS IN CASE OF ATTACK

Law enforcement has a number of mind-numbing issues when the discussion of dirty bombs comes up: neighborhood watches, better communications with community civil and religious leaders, better monitoring of any local utility or business that may harbor even the smallest amounts of radioactive material.

Kelly also pointed out in his report that early detection should be key in trying to prevent a dirty bomb scenario. "Systems capable of detecting dangerous amounts of radiation are comparatively inexpensive and unobtrusive." The Office of Homeland Security did in fact identify the areas where such sensors were needed and had as many installed as they possibly could. As the 2003 New Year's Eve scenario illustrated, Tom Ridge's department took Kelly's words to heart. Transportation systems such as airports, harbors, rail stations, tunnels, and highways were monitored. Scrap-metal yards and landfill sites were also targeted.

Kelly also spoke of properly educating and equipping first responder emergency departments in case of a dirty bomb attack. "First responders and hospital personnel need to understand how to protect themselves and affected citizens in the event of a radiological attack and be able to rapidly determine if individuals have been exposed to radiation."

UPDATING EQUIPMENT

Acquiring such new products as radiation detectors to help law enforcement and other security organizations is of paramount importance in major cities since 9/11. The most famous of these products is the ten-pound Cryo3, announced in 2002, the result of a joint effort by Los Alamos, Lawrence Berkeley, and Lawrence Livermore labs, and appearing in *Popular Mechanics*.

"It was the first handheld radiation detector, not only allowing security personnel to quickly check for radiation anywhere, but also to determine the exact amount and type," reported popularmechanics.com. "Gamma and X rays emitted from so-called dirty bombs interact with a high-purity geranium crystal at the unit's core to create a unique charge, which is analyzed by a computer to determine the radioactive isotope."

The private sector rose to the occasion too. In January of 2004, Radiation Shield Technologies (RST) announced an entire dirty bomb line, Demron, specifically designed for such an attack.

"The new product line uses Demron™, a radiation protective fabric created with nanotechnology. The material is lightweight, non-toxic and lead-free," reported PRNewswire. "Demron™ . . . can effectively shield the human body from ionizing radiation. The material has been tested and confirmed to be an effective shield against radiation by the U.S. Department of Energy and other institutions."

RST created a line of radiation protective tactical vests, suppression blankets, and full body suits. Tactical vests protect vital organs from harmful radiation, allowing responders to remain in a contaminated area at the height of an emergency. Suppression blankets are placed over an undetonated dirty bomb or radiological dispersal device (RDD). "The blanket is strong, durable, and is designed to reduce emissions from high energy gamma sources such as Cesium 137," reported PRNewswire. "The full body suit is useful in providing shielding while escaping a dirty bomb."

"We designed this new product line with the idea of protecting first responders against a dirty bomb or other radiological dispersal device," stated Dr. DeMeo, CEO of RST. "The tactical vest allows first responders to move unencumbered, giving them the ability to rescue victims and fulfill their duties in the event of a radiological emergency."

VIGILANT SECURITY

Certainly, if we are going to be outfitting our police and security organizations with new, updated equipment, that equipment is only as good as those who are using it. It is imperative that those who are responsible for watching our nation's borders, entry points, and major transportation arteries be constantly aware that the time we least expect Al Qaeda is when Al Qaeda will most likely strike.

On September 11, 2003, with the Office of Home Security having already placed the country on high alert, "A 'suspicious package' was positioned at the base of the famous Washington Monument, near the White House, on the second anniversary of September 11," reported an Irish news agency. "But police were busy chatting rather than patrolling the area and one officer positioned in an unmarked car appeared to be asleep." Luckily, this was a test. *The Washington Post* and CNN broke the story on January 13, 2004, citing an unpublished Department of the Interior report. According to reports, the package sat in plain view for twenty minutes.

Newswires quoted the report: "There was not a single security or law enforcement official who, in that time, came around to the rear of the monument." Investigators took an empty black bag and placed it conspicuously toward the front of the monument. It sat there undetected for another fifteen minutes. Park police failed again to notice the bag. According to a Scottish newspaper that carried the story as well, "The report claimed the security lapses caused investigators to 'question the value and purpose (of the police).'"

Since the incident, security has been tightened at the monument as well as at other nationally significant sites. It is not known if there have been other failed inspections.

EXPERIMENTING AND TESTING 'DIRTY BOMBS'

It was revealed in March 2003 that in an effort to understand the effects of the crudely made dirty bomb explosion, the United States and Russia were testing its blast patterns and radiological effects. Scientists from both sides let it be known that they had detonated several bombs, in the New Mexican desert and Ural Mountains, respectively, the Sandia National Laboratories for more than six months.

One of the most important findings was that the radiological patterns were not as had been speculated. "Radioactive particles from an explosion do not disperse in an oval pattern following wind direction, as usually theorized, but in a much more irregular pattern affected by crosscurrents," announced the Associated Press.

The report was released in March 2003 at an international conference attended by some 600 scientists and government officials that "focused on tightening protection of radioisotopes in use worldwide, stopping illicit trafficking and planning emergency responses to such attacks," according to AP.

The conference was an eye-opener, with officials from all over the world trading information, some of which was released to the press. One U.S. official admitted that "A Russian admiral told us there have been many attempted thefts of Radiothermal Generators reported." According to the official, none had been successful.

Even though the attendees did not go into too much detail, the conference itself and related papers were deemed classified, other than official press releases. And all they reported was that the two governments were exchanging information and sharing their findings with appropriate international security officials worldwide.

"We are seeing adverse health effects among the entire group of warriors exposed during combat in Iraq, Saudi Arabia and Kuwait (and) civilians exposed in Iraq."

—Douglas Rokke

CHAPTER 9:

DIRTY SECRETS, DIRTY BOMBS: U.S. AND RUSSIA

DEPLETED URANIUM WEAPONS: WHY, HOW, AND WHEN—THE BENEFITS

With the concern over a dirty bomb attack growing more every day, the concern about how to rid the environment of dangerous radioactive materials left over from such a strike is also growing. Cleanup, indeed, would be the most costly and drawn-out aspect of the process of dealing with such a device. After all, who would want their child growing up in an area where radiation levels might be high? And wouldn't new parents naturally want to stay away from such places, fearful that radiation levels like that might cause birth defects of one sort or another? And how about adults? Long-term exposure might lead to cancer of different kinds. These are the fears people in Iraq, Chechnya, and the Balkans face every day.

The first dirty bomb was created by Iraq in 1987. The Iraqi military tested a one-ton radiological bomb. However, Iraq gave up on this program "because the radiation levels it generated were not deadly enough," according to an ABC News report.

Dirty bombs have since been used in war. They were first invented, tested, and used by the United States. And the United States uses bombs, armor-piercing shells, and armor-piercing bullets tipped with depleted uranium as well, a fact confirmed by such august news organizations such as the BBC, the *New York Times*, and *Harper's*.

What is "depleted uranium"? It is a waste product. It comes from producing fuel for nuclear reactors and nuclear weapons. "The material used in civil and nuclear military industry is uranium U-235, the isotope which can be fissioned," according to "'Depleted' Uranium Burning: An Eternal Medical Disaster," a website devoted to the subject. "Since this isotope is found in very low proportions in nature, the uranium ore has to be enriched, i.e., its proportion of the U-235 isotope has to be industrially increased. This process produces a large amount of radioactive depleted uranium waste, thus named because it is mainly formed by the other non-fissionable uranium isotope, U-238 and a minimum proportion of U-235."

According to some sources, the American military has been using depleted uranium in Tomahawk missiles since 1977, and as a component of navigational instruments. It was also used in the armor on our tanks and airplanes. And testing with shell casings began in the late 1980s.

Why use depleted uranium? On the tip of a shell, depleted uranium sharpens itself as it penetrates the armor. When an explosive charge detonates, depleted uranium becomes incendiary. And it is the perfect armor-piercing metal. Tungsten, which is far more expensive than depleted uranium and more difficult to find, does not penetrate as well, nor does it possess the same incendiary properties.

Tungsten also is a harder metal to work with.

"This type of weapon can penetrate many meters of reinforced concrete or rock in seconds," wrote Robert James Parsons for Le Monde Diplomatique. "The DU burns fiercely and rapidly, carbonizing everything in the void, while the DU itself is transformed into a fine uranium oxide powder. Although only 30% of the DU of a 30mm penetrator round is oxidized, the DU charge of a missile oxidizes 100%. Most of the dust particles produced measure less than 1.5 microns, small enough to be breathed in."

Such bombs can render tanks, bomb shelters, or underground military bunkers where weapons are cacheted immediately useless. They proved their worth in numerous operations. The U.S. and NATO used them in 1991 in the first Gulf War, in the Balkans, Somalia, and Afghanistan, and in the second Gulf War. It is also well known that the Russian military has its own version of such weapons and has used them against Chechen rebels.

The Pentagon briefed journalists about DU weapons in the spring of 2003.

"In the last war, Iraqi tanks at fairly close ranges – not nose to nose – fired at our tanks and the shot bounced off the heavy armor . . . and our shot did not bounce off their armor," Colonel James Naughton of U.S. Army Materiel Command told the briefing. "So the result was Iraqi tanks destroyed – U.S. tanks with scrape marks." The case for DU was made.

While the tank-penetrating rounds are, relatively speaking, light, the bunker busters can be devastating. Raytheon's bunker buster (a.k.a. GBU-28) weighs one and a half metric tones. That's a lot of oxidized DU floating in the air.

DU IS CONTROVERSIAL

There is no clear consensus on depleted uranium's potential for harming humans. The United Nations Environmental Program (UNEP) and the World Health Organization (WHO) released reports in March and April of 2001 claiming they could find no ill effects due to the amount of depleted uranium in regions where the weapons were used. The Pentagon agrees. They point to their own studies as well as pointing out that the United Nations is no friend of the U.S. military, and that these independent reports back up U.S. military's findings.

On January 12, 2001, Steven Erlanger, in a *New York Times* story "Uranium Furor Puts Kosovars in the Dark Again," wrote that "NATO is only now beginning to disclose sites in Kosovo that it bombed with weapons reinforced by depleted uranium and to consider cleaning up whatever debris might be left." Erlanger went on about how the people of Kosovo were barely consulted about the issues facing them. He also pointed out that World Health Organization said it had seen no increase in the incidence of leukemia among the population of Kosovo.

In a follow-up story for the *Times*, Marlise Simons reported that the Swiss Federal Institute of Technology confirmed that uranium isotopes were found is U.S. munitions, saying that "quantities found of uranium 235 were minute."

Harper's also carried the story, reporting, "Swiss researchers found traces of uranium 236, which comes from nuclear fuel and nuclear waste, in samples of American-made depleted uranium found in Kosovo, raising concerns that the weapons debris might contain contaminants that are even more dangerous, such as plutonium and americium. NATO again said there was nothing to worry about."

But further investigations have brought UNEP's and WHO's findings into question. The UNEP teams searching for sites were guided by NATO teams. According to some investigations, the "NATO troops prevented researchers from any contact with DU sub-munitions, even from discovering their existence," reported Parsons. "During the 16 months before the UNEP mission, the Pentagon sent at least 10 study teams into the field and did major clean-up operations. Out of 8,112 anti-tank penetrator rounds fired on the sites studied, the UNEP team recovered only 11. . . . And . . . the amount of dust found directly on sites hit by these rounds was particularly small." And, upon further investigation, he found that the WHO study was not a field study, but had been restricted by the International Atomic Energy Agency (IAEA) to study DU as a heavy metal and chemical contaminant only.

Similar stories are now coming out of Iraq as well. "During the Gulf War, munitions and armor made with depleted uranium were used for the first time in a military action," wrote Ramsey Clark, former U.S. attorney general, in a statement titled "An International Appeal to Ban the Use of Depleted Uranium Weapons." "Iraq and northern Kuwait were a virtual testing range for depleted-uranium weapons. Over 940,000 30-millimeter uranium tipped bullets and 'more than 14,000 large caliber DU rounds were consumed during Operation Desert Storm/Desert Shield' (U.S. Army Environmental Policy Institute)." According to Clark, between three hundred and eight hundred tons of depleted uranium dust particles were scattered on the ground and in the water of Kuwait, Saudi Arabia, and Iraq.

It was also reported in January 2001 that the U.S. had used DU weapons in Mogadishu. Der Spiegel presented evidence from the United States General Army headquarters, in a communication for the medical personnel: "Among the members of the U.S. force, there may be cases of contamination, especially among those who were exposed in an exceptional way to depleted uranium".

German defense minister Rudolf Scharping went public, saying their U.S. counterparts had not informed them of the use of DU weapons at the time. He was so "furious about this, the German Minister could not hide his anger when he remembered that the USA had also used plutonium weapons in the Balkans without warning their allies. 'A friendly nation must inform its partners, for God's sake!' he said as he began a two-day visit to the German troops stationed in the Balkans."

"Perhaps the most extraordinary official endorsement of depleted uranium's benign nature came from former Secretary of Defense William Cohen, who once deemed it as safe as 'leaded paint,'" wrote Elliot Borin for *Wired* magazine. Borin further noted: "Federal law has banned the use of leaded paint in residential structures since 1978 because of its extreme toxicity."

GULF WAR SYNDROME

According to a host of experts at the International Action Center (IAC), a foundation set up to fight the use of depleted uranium weapons, scores of experts have written letters advocating discontinuing the DU weapons program. Many point out that hundreds, even thousands, of people, including combatants and civilians, have shown symptoms of suffering from varying degrees of radiation exposure due to radioactive weapons.

With Gulf War Syndrome such a huge topic, the president commissioned a study on the causes of this stressful condition. The "Presidential Advisory Committee on Gulf War Veteran's Illnesses: Final Report: December 1996" stated: "The Committee concludes it is unlikely that health effects reported by Gulf War veterans today are the result of exposure to DU during the Gulf War. Since uranium is a potential carcinogen, it is possible that exposure to DU during the Gulf War could lead to a slight increase in the risk for lung cancer after decades following the end of the war."

According to Ramsey Clark and the IAC, 90,000 veterans of the first Gulf War out of the 697,000 who served have reported some medical concern. Respiratory problems, kidney and liver dysfunction, headaches, and low blood pressure are all conditions associated with excessive radiation exposure. So is a high rate of birth defects in newborns. Even the advisory commission noted, "The chemical toxicity of uranium as a heavy metal is well characterized. In fact, the kidney is the most sensitive organ affected by exposure to uranium and is the critical target organ for risk assessment."

"DU is a leading suspect for a portion of these ailments," writes Clark. "The effects on the population living in Iraq are far greater. Under pressure, the Pentagon has been forced to acknowledge Gulf War Syndrome, but they are still stonewalling any connection to DU."

Iraqi citizens have also experienced many of the same symptoms. "Iraqi doctors have found high levels of leukemia and other cancers and birth defects in the areas where DU was most used during the war," reported John Catalinotto for the IAC. "In addition, about 100,000 U.S. troops have experienced symptoms categorized as the Gulf War Syndrome, which may be at least partially caused by DU."

"Since 1990, the incident rate of leukemia in Iraq has grown by more than 600 percent," stated *Counterpunch* magazine, "DU: Cancer as a Weapon," on February 5, 2001. "The situation is compounded by Iraq's forced isolations and the sadistic sanctions regime, recently described by UN secretary-general Kofi Annan as 'a humanitarian crisis,' that makes detection and treatment of the cancers all the more difficult."

"A 1991 study by the UK Atomic Energy Authority predicted that if less than 10 percent of the particles released by depleted uranium weapons used in Iraq and Kuwait were inhaled it could result in as many as '300,000 probable deaths,'" *Counterpunch* reported. As they pointed out, these deductions were based on assumptions that the only thing in the U.S. bombs was only DU. That was a mistake. "A new study of the materials inside these weapons describes them as a 'nuclear cocktail,' containing a mix of radioactive elements, including plutonium and the highly radioactive isotope uranium-236. These elements are 100,000 times more dangerous than depleted uranium."

However, the most damning admission comes from one of the Army's own. Physicist Douglas Rokke was sent to Iraq in 1991 to study the effects of the more than three hundred tons of DU weapons that veterans were exposed to during the war.

"In the mid-1990s, he was recalled to active duty and made director of a project intended to develop training and management procedures for handling depleted uranium contamination," wrote Elliot Borin in *Wired*. Rokke told him, "We are seeing adverse health effects among the entire group of warriors exposed during combat in Iraq, Saudi Arabia and Kuwait (and) civilians exposed in Iraq."

Rokke admitted that they were also seeing similar findings at U.S. and foreign installations where there was DU testing and training.

BALKAN SYNDROME

Another hot story in the European press was that a new illness was plaguing UN Peace Keeping veterans of the Balkans, an international coalition dispatched to the former Yugoslavia to keep the peace after the bombings in Kosovo, Bosnia, and Serbia. Again, NATO forces had used bunker busters and antitank bombs and shells to pierce heavy armor.

"Over a dozen have died of leukemia; many suffer chronic fatigue, hair loss, and various forms of cancer," Roger D. Hodge reported in *Harper's*. "Exposure to depleted uranium, which was used in NATO's bombings . . . was thought to be responsible. A NATO spokesman denied that depleted uranium was a significant hazard, though the U.S. Department of Transportation, which has used the metal to balance aircraft, warns personnel that the material is extremely hazardous if particles are ingested or inhaled, something particularly likely after a bombing, which produces large quantities of depleted-uranium dust."

The IAC also ran a story on October 4, 2000, that Portugal had notified NATO that it wanted its troops withdrawn from Kosovo because it felt its troops' health would be endangered by DU ammunition.

According to *Diario de Noticias*, a Portuguese newspaper, the Portuguese defense minister Castro Caldas complained that he had not been warned by NATO's general secretary before sending his troops into the region of Kosovo that had been especially contaminated by DU shells. Later governmental denials claimed that the Portuguese needed to withdraw their troops to quell problems in East Timor, a former colony.

CONCLUSION

It's obvious that there needs to be a lot more independent research done on depleted uranium weapons. It seems that the U.S. Army and NATO are holding fast to the idea that they have no hard evidence from any other government or government's army that refutes their claims. And few weapons manufacturers are going to blow the whistle on some of their biggest sellers.

It also has to be remembered that TNT, black powder, dynamite, and other explosives are not good for any soldier's health either, whether in the mixing, storing, or detonating stages. And the battlefield is filled with all kinds of carcinogens, whether from shell casings, grenades and bombs. But reviewing what is known about dirty bombs from all the intelligence out there, the real question is: If a terrorist's dirty bomb is so dangerous to emergency workers, first responders, and civilians, then why aren't depleted uranium weapons?

APPENDIX

LIST OF NUCLEAR FACILITIES AROUND THE WORLD

According to the *Bulletin of the Atomic Scientist*'s most up-to-date statistics, "as of December 1998, 429 nuclear reactors were operating around the world, producing more than 345 billion watts (345 GWe) of electricity. There are also 30 reactors currently under construction, mostly in Asia, which combined are expected to produce an additional 22 GWe." The 429 reactors are those used to supply power to people all over the world. According to the reactor industry, nuclear power makes up only 10 percent of the world's energy supply. Fossil fuels account for the other 90 percent: 36 percent from oil, 36 percent from gas, and 18 percent from coal. All fossil fuels must be burned to generate consumable energy.

There are another 550 "research reactors" around the world. "Most are relatively small and mainly used for research and training purposes," claims the Bulletin. "They do not produce energy for public consumption."

Of the 429 reactors around the world, 25 percent are in the United States. But these 107 reactors supply less than 20 percent of U.S. energy overall. "In contrast, France produces 78 percent of its electricity through fission; other leaders include Belgium (60 percent) and Lithuania (82 percent)," the Bulletin states further.

Approximately 75 percent of the 429 reactors are pressurized-water reactors and boiling-water reactors. In Eastern Europe and the former Soviet Union, there are thirteen of these RBMK reactors operating (the same reactor used at Chernobyl).

The security measures taken in and around nuclear reactors have been one of the major initiatives for the Homeland Security Commission. However, there are concerns that elsewhere in the world officials are not being serious enough about the threat of theft from such facilities. While nuclear weapons cannot be made from the spent fuel rods, certainly the radiation from that rod or other discarded part could help bring a dirty bomb scenario to fruition.

Facility Name	Process	Status
AGESTA, Sweden	HWR	Shut down
Aguirre, United States	PWR	Suspended indefinitely/Canceled
Aktash-1, Ukraine	PWR/VVER	Suspended indefinitely/Canceled
Aktash-2, Ukraine	PWR/VVER	Suspended indefinitely/Canceled
Allens Creek-1, United States	BWR	Suspended indefinitely/Canceled
Allens Creek-2, United States	BWR	Suspended indefinitely/Canceled
Almaraz-1, Spain	PWR	Operating
Almaraz-2, Spain	PWR	Operating
Angra-1, Brazil	PWR	Operating
Angra-2, Brazil	PWR	Operating
Apulia-1, Italy	PWR	Suspended indefinitely/Canceled
Apulia-2, Italy	PWR	Suspended indefinitely/Canceled
Argonne EBWR, United States	BWR	Shut down
Arkansas Nuclear One-1, United States	PWR	Operating
Arkansas Nuclear One-2, United States	PWR	Operating
Armenia-1 (Metsamor), Armenia	PWR/VVER	Shut down
Armenia-2 (Metsamor), Armenia	PWR/VVER	Operating
Asco-1, Spain	PWR	Operating
Asco-2, Spain	PWR	Operating
Ashihama-1, Japan	BWR	Suspended indefinitely/Canceled
Ashihama-2, Japan	BWR	Suspended indefinitely/Canceled
Atlantic-1, United States	PWR	Suspended indefinitely/Canceled
Atlantic-2, United States	PWR	Suspended indefinitely/Canceled
Atlantic-3, United States	PWR	Suspended indefinitely/Canceled
Atlantic-4, United States	PWR	Suspended indefinitely/Canceled
Atucha-1, Argentina	PHWR	Operating
Atucha-2, Argentina	PHWR	Suspended indefinitely/Canceled
Bailly, United States	BWR	Suspended indefinitely/Canceled
Balakovo-1, Russian Federation	PWR/VVER	Operating
Balakovo-2, Russian Federation	PWR/VVER	Operating
Balakovo-3, Russian Federation	PWR/VVER	Operating
Balakovo-4, Russian Federation	PWR/VVER	Operating
Balakovo-5, Russian Federation	PWR/VVER	Suspended indefinitely/Canceled
Balakovo-6, Russian Federation	PWR/VVER	Suspended indefinitely/Canceled
Barsebaeck-1, Sweden	BWR	Shut down
Barsebaeck-2, Sweden	BWR	Operating
Barton-1, United States	BWR	Suspended indefinitely/Canceled
Barton-2, United States	BWR	Suspended indefinitely/Canceled
Barton-3, United States	BWR	Suspended indefinitely/Canceled
Barton-4, United States	BWR	Suspended indefinitely/Canceled
Bashkir-1, Russian Federation	PWR/VVER	Suspended indefinitely/Canceled
Bashkir-2, Russian Federation	PWR/VVER	Suspended indefinitely/Canceled
Bashkir-3, Russian Federation	PWR/VVER	Suspended indefinitely/Canceled
Bayside, United States	BWR	Suspended indefinitely/Canceled
Beaver Valley-1, United States	PWR	Operating

Beaver Valley-2, United States	PWR	Operating
Belene-1, Bulgaria	PWR/VVER	Suspended indefinitely/Canceled
Belene-2, Bulgaria	PWR/VVER	Suspended indefinitely/Canceled
Belene-3, Bulgaria	PWR/VVER	Suspended indefinitely/Canceled
Belene-4, Bulgaria	PWR/VVER	Suspended indefinitely/Canceled
Bellefonte-1, United States	PWR	Suspended indefinitely/Canceled
Bellefonte-2, United States	PWR	Suspended indefinitely/Canceled
Belleville-1, France	PWR	Operating
Belleville-2, France	PWR	Operating
Beloyarsky-1, Russian Federation	LWGR/RBMK	Shut down
Beloyarsky-2, Russian Federation	LWGR/RBMK	Shut down
Beloyarsky-3 (BN-600), Russian Fed.	FBR	Operating
Beloyarsky-4 (BN-800), Russian Fed.	FBR	Under construction
Berkeley-1, United Kingdom	GCR	Shut down
Berkeley-2, United Kingdom	GCR	Shut down
Beznau-1, Switzerland	PWR	Operating
Beznau-2, Switzerland	PWR	Operating
Biblis-A, Germany	PWR	Operating
Biblis-B, Germany	PWR	Operating
Biblis-C, Germany	PWR	Suspended indefinitely/Canceled
Big Rock Point, United States	BWR	Shut down
Bilibino unit A, Russian Federation	LWGR/EGP	Opérating
Bilibino unit B, Russian Federation	LWGR/EGP	Operating
Bilibino unit C, Russian Federation	LWGR/EGP	Operating
Bilibino unit D, Russian Federation	LWGR/EGP	Operating
Black Fox-1, United States	BWR	Suspended indefinitely/Canceled
Black Fox-2, United States	BWR	Suspended indefinitely/Canceled
Blayais-1, France	PWR	Operating
Blayais-2, France	PWR	Operating
Blayais-3, France	PWR	Operating
Blayais-4, France	PWR	Operating
Blue Hills-1, United States	PWR	Suspended indefinitely/Canceled
Blue Hills-2, United States	PWR	Suspended indefinitely/Canceled
BN-350 Aktau (Shevchenko), Kazakhstan	LMFBR	Shut down
Bodega Bay, United States	BWR	Suspended indefinitely/Canceled
Bohunice A-1, Slovak Republic	HWGCR	Shut down
Bohunice-1, Slovak Republic	PWR/VVER	Operating
Bohunice-2, Slovak Republic	PWR/VVER	Operating
Bohunice-3, Slovak Republic	PWR/VVER	Operating
Bohunice-4, Slovak Republic	PWR/VVER	Operating
Bonus (Demo), United States	BWR	Shut down
Borken, Germany	PWR	Suspended indefinitely/Canceled
Borssele, Netherlands	PWR	Operating
BR-3 PWR (test), Belgium	PWR	Shut down
Bradwell Unit A, United Kingdom	GCR	Shut down
Bradwell Unit B, United Kingdom	GCR	Shut down

Braidwood-1, United States	PWR	Operating
Braidwood-2, United States	PWR	Operating
Brokdorf, Germany	PWR	Operating
Browns Ferry-1, United States	BWR	Not operating
Browns Ferry-2, United States	BWR	Operating
Browns Ferry-3, United States	BWR	Operating
Bruce-1, Canada	PHWR/CANDU	Not operating
Bruce-2, Canada	PHWR/CANDU	Not operating
Bruce-3, Canada	PHWR/CANDU	Operating
Bruce-4, Canada	PHWR/CANDU	Operating
Bruce-5, Canada	PHWR/CANDU	Operating
Bruce-6, Canada	PHWR/CANDU	Operating
Bruce-7, Canada	PHWR/CANDU	Operating
Bruce-8, Canada	PHWR/CANDU	Operating
Brunsbuttel, Germany	BWR	Operating
Brunswick-1, United States	BWR	Operating
Brunswick-2, United States	BWR	Operating
Bugey-1, France	GCR	Shut down
Bugey-2, France	PWR	Operating
Bugey-3, France	PWR	Operating
Bugey-4, France	PWR	Operating
Bugey-5, France	PWR	Operating
Bushehr-1, Iran	PWR/VVER	Under construction
Byron-1, United States	PWR	Operating
Byron-2, United States	PWR	Operating
Cabo Cope-1, Spain	BWR	Suspended indefinitely/Canceled
Calder Hall-1, United Kingdom	GCR	Shut down
Calder Hall-2, United Kingdom	GCR	Shut down
Calder Hall-3, United Kingdom	GCR	Shut down
Calder Hall-4, United Kingdom	GCR	Shut down
Callaway-1, United States	PWR	Operating
Callaway-2, United States	PWR	Suspended indefinitely/Canceled
Calvert Cliffs-1, United States	PWR	Operating
Calvert Cliffs-2, United States	PWR	Operating
Caorso, Italy	BWR	Shut down
Carolinas CVTR, United States	PHWR	Shut down
Carroll County-1, United States	PWR	Suspended indefinitely/Canceled
Carroll County-2, United States	PWR	Suspended indefinitely/Canceled
Catawba-1, United States	PWR	Operating
Catawba-2, United States	PWR	Operating
Cattenom-1, France	PWR	Operating
Cattenom-2, France	PWR	Operating
Cattenom-3, France	PWR	Operating
Cattenom-4, France	PWR	Operating
Central Iowa, United States	PWR	Suspended indefinitely/Canceled
Cernavoda-1, Romania	PHWR/CANDU	Operating

Cernavoda-2, Romania	PHWR	Under construction
Cernavoda-3, Romania	PHWR	Suspended indefinitely/Canceled
Cernavoda-4, Romania	PHWR	Suspended indefinitely/Canceled
Cernavoda-5, Romania	PHWR	Suspended indefinitely/Canceled
Chapelcross-1, United Kingdom	GCR	Operating
Chapelcross-2, United Kingdom	GCR	Operating
Chapelcross-3, United Kingdom	GCR	Operating
Chapelcross-4, United Kingdom	GCR	Operating
Charlestown-1, United States	PWR	Suspended indefinitely/Canceled
Charlestown-2, United States	PWR	Suspended indefinitely/Canceled
Chasnupp-1, Pakistan	PWR	Operating
Chernobyl-1, Ukraine	LWGR/RBMK	Shut down
Chernobyl-2, Ukraine	LWGR/RBMK	Shut down
Chernobyl-3, Ukraine	LWGR/RBMK	Shut down
Chernobyl-4, Ukraine	LWGR/RBMK	Shut down
Chernobyl-5, Ukraine	LWGR/RBMK	Suspended indefinitely/Canceled
Chernobyl-6, Ukraine	LWGR/RBMK	Suspended indefinitely/Canceled
Cherokee-1, United States	PWR	Suspended indefinitely/Canceled
Cherokee-2, United States	PWR	Suspended indefinitely/Canceled
Cherokee-3, United States	PWR	Suspended indefinitely/Canceled
Chin Shan-1, China, Greater	BWR	Operating
Chin Shan-2, China, Greater	BWR	Operating
Chinon-1, France	GCR	Shut down
Chinon-2, France	GCR	Shut down
Chinon-3, France	GCR	Shut down
Chinon-B1, France	PWR	Operating
Chinon-B2, France	PWR	Operating
Chinon-B3, France	PWR	Operating
Chinon-B4, France	PWR	Operating
Chooz-A (Prototype), France	PWR	Shut down
Chooz-B1, France	PWR	Operating
Chooz-B2, France	PWR	Operating
Cirene, Italy	HWLWR	Suspended indefinitely/Canceled
Civaux-1, France	PWR	Operating
Civaux-2, France	PWR	Operating
Clinch River, United States	FBR	Suspended indefinitely/Canceled
Clinton-1, United States	BWR	Operating
Clinton-2, United States	BWR	Suspended indefinitely/Canceled
Cofrentes, Spain	BWR	Operating
Columbia (WNP-2), United States	BWR	Operating
Comanche Peak-1, United States	PWR	Operating
Comanche Peak-2, United States	PWR	Operating
Cooper, United States	BWR	Operating
Cruas-1, France	PWR	Operating
Cruas-2, France	PWR	Operating
Cruas-3, France	PWR	Operating

Cruas-4, France	PWR	Operating
Crystal River-3, United States	PWR	Operating
Crystal River-4, United States	PWR	Suspended indefinitely/Canceled
Dampierre-1, France	PWR	Operating
Dampierre-2, France	PWR	Operating
Dampierre-3, France	PWR	Operating
Dampierre-4, France	PWR	Operating
Darlington-1, Canada	PHWR/CANDU	Operating
Darlington-2, Canada	PHWR/CANDU	Operating
Darlington-3, Canada	PHWR/CANDU	Operating
Darlington-4, Canada	PHWR/CANDU	Operating
Davis Besse-1, United States	PWR	Operating
Davis Besse-2, United States	PWR	Suspended indefinitely/Canceled
Davis Besse-3, United States	PWR	Suspended indefinitely/Canceled
Diablo Canyon-1, United States	PWR	Operating
Diablo Canyon-2, United States	PWR	Operating
Doel-1, Belgium	PWR	Operating
Doel-2, Belgium	PWR	Operating
Doel-3, Belgium	PWR	Operating
Doel-4, Belgium	PWR	Operating
Donald Cook-1, United States	PWR	Operating
Donald Cook-2, United States	PWR	Operating
Douglas Point (Prototype), Canada	PHWR/CANDU	Shut down
Douglas Point-1, United States	BWR	Suspended indefinitely/Canceled
Douglas Point-2, United States	BWR	Suspended indefinitely/Canceled
Dounreay DFR, United Kingdom	FBR	Shut down
Dounreay PFR, United Kingdom	FBR	Shut down
Dresden-1, United States	BWR	Shut down
Dresden-2, United States	BWR	Operating
Dresden-3, United States	BWR	Operating
Duane Arnold-1, United States	BWR	Operating
Dukovany-1, Czech Republic	PWR/VVER	Operating
Dukovany-2, Czech Republic	PWR/VVER	Operating
Dukovany-3, Czech Republic	PWR/VVER	Operating
Dukovany-4, Czech Republic	PWR/VVER	Operating
Dungeness-A1, United Kingdom	GCR	Operating
Dungeness-A2, United Kingdom	GCR	Operating
Dungeness-B1, United Kingdom	AGR	Operating
Dungeness-B2, United Kingdom	AGR	Operating
EBR-II (test), United States	FBR	Shut down
EL-4 (Prototype), France	HWGCR	Shut down
Elk River, United States	BWR	Shut down
Embalse, Argentina	PHWR	Operating
Emsland, Germany	PWR	Operating
Enrico Fermi-1, United States	FBR	Shut down
Enrico Fermi-2, United States	BWR	Operating

Enrico Fermi-3, United States	BWR	Suspended indefinitely/Canceled
Erie-1, United States	PWR	Suspended indefinitely/Canceled
Erie-2, United States	PWR	Suspended indefinitely/Canceled
Escatron-1, Spain	PWR	Suspended indefinitely/Canceled
Escatron-2, Spain	PWR	Suspended indefinitely/Canceled
Farley-1, United States	PWR	Operating
Farley-2, United States	PWR	Operating
Fessenheim-1, France	PWR	Operating
Fessenheim-2, France	PWR	Operating
Fitzpatrick, United States	BWR	Operating
Flamanville-1, France	PWR	Operating
Flamanville-2, France	PWR	Operating
Forsmark-1, Sweden	BWR	Operating
Forsmark-2, Sweden	BWR	Operating
Forsmark-3, Sweden	BWR	Operating
Fort Calhoun-1, United States	PWR	Operating
Fort Calhoun-2, United States	PWR	Suspended indefinitely/Canceled
Fort St Vrain, United States	HTGR	Shut down
Fugen ATR, Japan	HWLWR	Shut down
Fukushima-Daiichi-1, Japan	BWR	Operating
Fukushima-Daiichi-2, Japan	BWR	Operating
Fukushima-Daiichi-3, Japan	BWR	Operating
Fukushima-Daiichi-4, Japan	BWR	Operating
Fukushima-Daiichi-5, Japan	BWR	Operating
Fukushima-Daiichi-6, Japan	BWR	Operating
Fukushima-Daiichi-7, Japan	ABWR	Under construction
Fukushima-Daiichi-8, Japan	ABWR	Under construction
Fukushima-Daini-1, Japan	BWR	Operating
Fukushima-Daini-2, Japan	BWR	Operating
Fukushima-Daini-3, Japan	BWR	Operating
Fukushima-Daini-4, Japan	BWR	Operating
G-2 (Marcoule), France	GCR	Shut down
G-3 (Marcoule), France	GCR	Shut down
Garigliano, Italy	BWR	Shut down
Genkai-1, Japan	PWR	Operating
Genkai-2, Japan	PWR	Operating
Genkai-3, Japan	PWR	Operating
Genkai-4, Japan	PWR	Operating
Gentilly-1 (Demo), Canada	HWLWR/CANDU	Shut down
Gentilly-2, Canada	PHWR/CANDU	Operating
GKN Dodewaard, Netherlands	BWR	Shut down
Goesgen, Switzerland	PWR	Operating
Golfech-1, France	PWR	Operating
Golfech-2, France	PWR	Operating
Gorky-1, Russian Federation	BWR	Suspended indefinitely/Canceled
Gorky-2, Russian Federation	BWR	Suspended indefinitely/Canceled

Grafenrheinfeld, Germany	PWR	Operating
Grand Gulf-1, United States	BWR	Operating
Grand Gulf-2, United States	BWR	Suspended indefinitely/Canceled
Gravelines-1, France	PWR	Operating
Gravelines-2, France	PWR	Operating
Gravelines-3, France	PWR	Operating
Gravelines-4, France	PWR	Operating
Gravelines-5, France	PWR	Operating
Gravelines-6, France	PWR	Operating
Greifswald-1, Germany	PWR/VVER	Shut down
Greifswald-2, Germany	PWR/VVER	Shut down
Greifswald-3, Germany	PWR/VVER	Shut down
Greifswald-4, Germany	PWR/VVER	Shut down
Greifswald-5, Germany	PWR/VVER	Shut down
Greifswald-6, Germany	PWR/VVER	Suspended indefinitely/Canceled
Greifswald-7, Germany	PWR/VVER	Suspended indefinitely/Canceled
Greifswald-8, Germany	PWR/VVER	Suspended indefinitely/Canceled
Grohnde, Germany	PWR	Operating
Grosswelzheim, Germany	BWR	Shut down
Guangdong-1 (Daya Bay 1), China	PWR	Operating
Guangdong-2 (Daya Bay 2), China	PWR	Operating
Gundremmingen KRB-A, Germany	BWR	Shut down
Gundremmingen-B, Germany	BWR	Operating
Gundremmingen-C, Germany	BWR	Operating
H B Robinson-2, United States	PWR	Operating
Haddam Neck, United States	PWR	Shut down
Hallam, United States	Na-graphite	Shut down
Hamaoka-1, Japan	BWR	Operating
Hamaoka-2, Japan	BWR	Operating
Hamaoka-3, Japan	BWR	Operating
Hamaoka-4, Japan	BWR	Operating
Hamaoka-5, Japan	ABWR	Under construction
Hartlepool-1, United Kingdom	AGR	Operating
Hartlepool-2, United Kingdom	AGR	Operating
Hartsville-A1, United States	BWR	Suspended indefinitely/Canceled
Hartsville-A2, United States	BWR	Suspended indefinitely/Canceled
Hatch-1, United States	BWR	Operating
Hatch-2, United States	BWR	Operating
Heysham-A1, United Kingdom	AGR	Operating
Heysham-A2, United Kingdom	AGR	Operating
Heysham-B1, United Kingdom	AGR	Operating
Heysham-B2, United Kingdom	AGR	Operating
Higashi-Dori-1, Japan	BWR	Under construction
Hinkley Point-A1, United Kingdom	GCR (Magnox)	Shut down
Hinkley Point-A2, United Kingdom	GCR (Magnox)	Shut down
Hinkley Point-B1, United Kingdom	AGR	Operating

Hinkley Point-B2, United Kingdom	AGR	Operating
Hope Creek-1, United States	BWR	Operating
Hope Creek-2, United States	BWR	Suspended indefinitely/Canceled
Humboldt Bay, United States	BWR	Shut down
Hunterston-A1, United Kingdom	GCR (Magnox)	Shut down
Hunterston-A2, United Kingdom	GCR (Magnox)	Shut down
Hunterston-B1, United Kingdom	AGR	Operating
Hunterston-B2, United Kingdom	AGR	Operating
Ignalina-1, Lithuania	LWGR/RBMK	Operating
Ignalina-2, Lithuania	LWGR/RBMK	Operating
Ignalina-3, Lithuania	LWGR/RBMK	Suspended indefinitely/Canceled
Ikata-1, Japan	PWR	Operating
Ikata-2, Japan	PWR	Operating
Ikata-3, Japan	PWR	Operating
Indian Point-1, United States	PWR	Shut down
Indian Point-2, United States	PWR	Operating
Indian Point-3, United States	PWR	Operating
Isar-1, Germany	BWR	Operating
Isar-2, Germany	PWR	Operating
Java-1, Indonesia	PWR	Planned
Jose Cabrera-1 (Zorita), Spain	PWR	Operating
JPDR-II, Japan	BWR	Shut down
Juelich AVR, Germany	HTGR	Shut down
Juragua-1, Cuba	PWR/VVER	Suspended indefinitely/Canceled
Juragua-2, Cuba	PWR/VVER	Suspended indefinitely/Canceled
Kahl VAK, Germany	BWR	Shut down
Kaiga-1, India	PHWR	Operating
Kaiga-2, India	PHWR	Operating
Kaiga-3, India	PHWR	Under construction
Kaiga-4, India	PHWR	Under construction
Kakrapar-1, India	PHWR	Operating
Kakrapar-2, India	PHWR	Operating
Kalinin-1, Russian Federation	PWR/VVER	Operating
Kalinin-2, Russian Federation	PWR/VVER	Operating
Kalinin-3, Russian Federation	PWR/VVER	Under construction
Kalinin-4, Russian Federation	PWR/VVER	Suspended indefinitely/Canceled
Kalkar (SN300), Germany	FBR	Suspended indefinitely/Canceled
Kalpakkam, India	FBR	Under construction
Kanupp, Pakistan	PHWR	Operating
Karlsruhe MZFR, Germany	PHWR	Shut down
Kashiwazaki Kariwa-1, Japan	BWR	Operating
Kashiwazaki Kariwa-2, Japan	BWR	Operating
Kashiwazaki Kariwa-3, Japan	BWR	Operating
Kashiwazaki Kariwa-4, Japan	BWR	Operating
Kashiwazaki Kariwa-5, Japan	BWR	Operating
Kashiwazaki Kariwa-6, Japan	ABWR	Operating

Kashiwazaki Kariwa-7, Japan	ABWR	Operating
Kewaunee, United States	PWR	Operating
Kharkov-1, Ukraine	PWR/VVER	Suspended indefinitely/Canceled
Khmelnitski-1, Ukraine	PWR/VVER	Operating
Khmelnitski-2, Ukraine	PWR/VVER	Under construction
Khmelnitski-3, Ukraine	PWR/VVER	Suspended indefinitely/Canceled
Khmelnitski-4, Ukraine	PWR/VVER	Suspended indefinitely/Canceled
KNK-II, Germany	FBR	Shut down
Koeberg-1, South Africa	PWR	Operating
Koeberg-2, South Africa	PWR	Operating
Kola-1, Russian Federation	PWR/VVER	Operating
Kola-2, Russian Federation	PWR/VVER	Operating
Kola-3, Russian Federation	PWR/VVER	Operating
Kola-4, Russian Federation	PWR/VVER	Operating
Koodankulam-1, India	PWR/VVER	Under construction
Koodankulam-2, India	PWR/VVER	Under construction
Kori-1, Korea RO (South)	PWR	Operating
Kori-2, Korea RO (South)	PWR	Operating
Kori-3, Korea RO (South)	PWR	Operating
Kori-4, Korea RO (South)	PWR	Operating
Kostroma-1, Russian Federation	PWR/VVER	Suspended indefinitely/Canceled
Kostroma-2, Russian Federation	PWR/VVER	Suspended indefinitely/Canceled
Kostroma-3, Russian Federation	PWR/VVER	Suspended indefinitely/Canceled
Kostroma-4, Russian Federation	PWR/VVER	Suspended indefinitely/Canceled
Kozloduy-1, Bulgaria	PWR/VVER	Shut down
Kozloduy-2, Bulgaria	PWR/VVER	Shut down
Kozloduy-3, Bulgaria	PWR/VVER	Operating
Kozloduy-4, Bulgaria	PWR/VVER	Operating
Kozloduy-5, Bulgaria	PWR/VVER	Operating
Kozloduy-6, Bulgaria	PWR/VVER	Operating
Krsko, Slovenia	PWR	Operating
Krummel, Germany	BWR	Operating
Kuosheng-1, China, Greater	BWR	Operating
Kuosheng-2, China, Greater	BWR	Operating
Kursk-1, Russian Federation	LWGR/RBMK	Operating
Kursk-2, Russian Federation	LWGR/RBMK	Operating
Kursk-3, Russian Federation	LWGR/RBMK	Operating
Kursk-4, Russian Federation	LWGR/RBMK	Operating
Kursk-5, Russian Federation	LWGR/RBMK	Under construction
Kursk-6, Russian Federation	LWGR/RBMK	Suspended indefinitely/Canceled
LaCrosse, United States	BWR	Shut down
Laguna Verde-1, Mexico	BWR	Operating
Laguna Verde-2, Mexico	BWR	Operating
LaSalle-1, United States	BWR	Operating
LaSalle-2, United States	BWR	Operating
Latina, Italy	GCR	Shut down

Leibstadt, Switzerland	BWR	Operating
Lemoniz-1, Spain	PWR	Suspended indefinitely/Canceled
Lemoniz-2, Spain	PWR	Suspended indefinitely/Canceled
Leningrad-1, Russian Federation	LWGR/RBMK	Operating
Leningrad-2, Russian Federation	LWGR/RBMK	Operating
Leningrad-3, Russian Federation	LWGR/RBMK	Operating
Leningrad-4, Russian Federation	LWGR/RBMK	Operating
Leningrad-5, Russian Federation	PWR/VVER	Suspended indefinitely/Canceled
Libya-1, Libya	PWR/VVER	Suspended indefinitely/Canceled
Limerick-1, United States	BWR	Operating
Limerick-2, United States	BWR	Operating
Lingao-1, China, Greater	PWR	Operating
Lingao-2, China, Greater	PWR	Operating
Lingen KWL, Germany	BWR	Shut down
Lombardy-1, Italy	PWR	Suspended indefinitely/Canceled
Lombardy-2, Italy	PWR	Suspended indefinitely/Canceled
Loviisa-1, Finland	PWR/VVER	Operating
Loviisa-2, Finland	PWR/VVER	Operating
Lucens CNL, Switzerland	HWGCR	Shut down
Lungmen-1, China, Greater	ABWR	Under construction
Lungmen-2, China, Greater	ABWR	Planned
Maanshan-1, China, Greater	PWR	Operating
Maanshan-2, China, Greater	PWR	Operating
Madras-1, India	PHWR	Operating
Madras-2, India	PHWR	Operating
Maine Yankee, United States	PWR	Shut down
Maki-1, Japan	BWR	Suspended indefinitely/Canceled
Marviken, Sweden		Suspended indefinitely/Canceled
McGuire-1, United States	PWR	Operating
McGuire-2, United States	PWR	Operating
Midland-1, United States	PWR	Suspended indefinitely/Canceled
Midland-2, United States	PWR	Suspended indefinitely/Canceled
Mihama-1, Japan	PWR	Operating
Mihama-2, Japan	PWR	Operating
Mihama-3, Japan	PWR	Operating
Millstone-1, United States	BWR	Shut down
Millstone-2, United States	PWR	Operating
Millstone-3, United States	PWR	Operating
Minsk-1, Belarus	PWR/VVER	Suspended indefinitely/Canceled
Mochovce-1, Slovak Republic	PWR/VVER	Operating
Mochovce-2, Slovak Republic	PWR/VVER	Operating
Mochovce-3, Slovak Republic	PWR/VVER	Under construction
Mochovce-4, Slovak Republic	PWR/VVER	Under construction
Monju, Japan	FBR	Not operating
Montalto di Castro-1, Italy	BWR	Suspended indefinitely/Canceled
Montalto di Castro-2, Italy	BWR	Suspended indefinitely/Canceled

Monticello, United States	BWR	Operating
Muehleberg, Switzerland	BWR	Operating
Muelheim-Karlich, Germany	PWR	Shut down
Namie-Odaka-1, Japan	BWR	Suspended indefinitely/Canceled
Narora-1, India	PHWR	Operating
Narora-2, India	PHWR	Operating
Neckarwestheim-1, Germany	PWR	Operating
Neckarwestheim-2, Germany	PWR	Operating
Neupotz-1, Germany	PWR	Suspended indefinitely/Canceled
Niederaichbach (KKN), Germany	HWGCR	Shut down
Nine Mile Point-1, United States	BWR	Operating
Nine Mile Point-2, United States	BWR	Operating
Nogent-1, France	PWR	Operating
Nogent-2, France	PWR	Operating
North Anna-1, United States	PWR	Operating
North Anna-2, United States	PWR	Operating
North Anna-3, United States	PWR	Suspended indefinitely/Canceled
North Anna-4, United States	PWR	Suspended indefinitely/Canceled
Novo Melekes (VK50), Russian Fed.	LWGR/RBMK	Shut down
Novovoronezh-1, Russian Federation	PWR/VVER	Shut down
Novovoronezh-2, Russian Federation	PWR/VVER	Shut down
Novovoronezh-3, Russian Federation	PWR/VVER	Shut down
Novovoronezh-4, Russian Federation	PWR/VVER	Operating
Novovoronezh-5, Russian Federation	PWR/VVER	Operating
Novovoronezh-6, Russian Federation	PWR/VVER	Planned
Obninsk APS (Prototype), Russian Fed.	LWGR	Shut down
Obrigheim, Germany	PWR	Operating
Oconee-1, United States	PWR	Operating
Oconee-2, United States	PWR	Operating
Oconee-3, United States	PWR	Operating
Odessa-1, Ukraine	PWR/VVER	Suspended indefinitely/Canceled
Odessa-2, Ukraine	PWR/VVER	Suspended indefinitely/Canceled
Ohi-1, Japan	PWR	Operating
Ohi-2, Japan	PWR	Operating
Ohi-3, Japan	PWR	Operating
Ohi-4, Japan	PWR	Operating
Ohma, Japan	ABWR	Planned
Ohma-Demonstration ATR, Japan	LWCHWR	Suspended indefinitely/Canceled
Oldbury-1, United Kingdom	GCR	Operating
Oldbury-2, United Kingdom	GCR	Operating
Olkiluoto-1, Finland	BWR	Operating
Olkiluoto-2, Finland	BWR	Operating
Olt, Romania	PWR/VVER	Suspended indefinitely/Canceled
Onagawa-1, Japan	BWR	Operating
Onagawa-2, Japan	BWR	Operating
Onagawa-3, Japan	BWR	Operating

Oskarshamn-1, Sweden	BWR	Operating
Oskarshamn-2, Sweden	BWR	Operating
Oskarshamn-3, Sweden	BWR	Operating
Oyster Creek, United States	BWR	Operating
Paks-1, Hungary	PWR	Operating
Paks-2, Hungary	PWR	Operating
Paks-3, Hungary	PWR	Operating
Paks-4, Hungary	PWR	Operating
Palisades, United States	PWR	Operating
Palo Verde-1, United States	PWR	Operating
Palo Verde-2, United States	PWR	Operating
Palo Verde-3, United States	PWR	Operating
Palo Verde-4, United States	PWR	Suspended indefinitely/Canceled
Palo Verde-5, United States	PWR	Suspended indefinitely/Canceled
Paluel-1, France	PWR	Operating
Paluel-2, France	PWR	Operating
Paluel-3, France	PWR	Operating
Paluel-4, France	PWR	Operating
Pathfinder test reactor, United States	BWR	Shut down
Peach Bottom-1, United States	HTGR	Shut down
Peach Bottom-2, United States	BWR	Operating
Peach Bottom-3, United States	BWR	Operating
Penly-1, France	PWR	Operating
Penly-2, France	PWR	Operating
Perry-1, United States	BWR	Operating
Perry-2, United States	BWR	Suspended indefinitely/Canceled
PFBR, India	FBR	Under construction
Phenix, France	FBR	Operating
Philippsburg-1, Germany	BWR	Operating
Philippsburg-2, Germany	PWR	Operating
Pickering-1, Canada	PHWR/CANDU	Not operating
Pickering-2, Canada	PHWR/CANDU	Not operating
Pickering-3, Canada	PHWR/CANDU	Not operating
Pickering-4, Canada	PHWR/CANDU	Not operating
Pickering-5, Canada	PHWR/CANDU	Operating
Pickering-6, Canada	PHWR/CANDU	Operating
Pickering-7, Canada	PHWR/CANDU	Operating
Pickering-8, Canada	PHWR/CANDU	Operating
Pilgrim-1, United States	BWR	Operating
Pilgrim-2, United States	PWR	Suspended indefinitely/Canceled
Pilgrim-3, United States	PWR	Suspended indefinitely/Canceled
Piqua, United States	OMR	Shut down
PNPP-1 (Batan), Philippines	PWR	Suspended indefinitely/Canceled
PNPP-2 (Batan), Philippines	PWR	Suspended indefinitely/Canceled
Point Beach-1, United States	PWR	Operating
Point Beach-2, United States	PWR	Operating

Point Lepreau, Canada	PHWR/CANDU	Operating
Prairie Island-1, United States	PWR	Operating
Prairie Island-2, United States	PWR	Operating
Qinshan-1, China, Greater	PWR	Operating
Qinshan-2, China, Greater	PWR	Operating
Qinshan-3, China, Greater	PWR	Under construction
Qinshan-4, China, Greater	PHWR/CANDU	Operating
Qinshan-5, China, Greater	PHWR/CANDU	Operating
Quad Cities-1, United States	BWR	Operating
Quad Cities-2, United States	BWR	Operating
R E Ginna, United States	PWR	Operating
Rajasthan-1, India	PHWR	Operating
Rajasthan-2, India	PHWR	Operating
Rajasthan-3, India	PHWR	Operating
Rajasthan-4, India	PHWR	Operating
Rajasthan-5, India	PHWR	Under construction
Rajasthan-6, India	PHWR	Under construction
Rancho Seco, United States	PWR	Shut down
Regodola-1, Spain	PWR	Suspended indefinitely/Canceled
Remerschen, Luxembourg	PWR	Suspended indefinitely/Canceled
Rheinsberg KKR, Germany	VVER	Shut down
Ringhals-1, Sweden	BWR	Operating
Ringhals-2, Sweden	PWR	Operating
Ringhals-3, Sweden	PWR	Operating
Ringhals-4, Sweden	PWR	Operating
River Bend-1, United States	BWR	Operating
River Bend-2, United States	BWR	Suspended indefinitely/Canceled
Rolphton NPD (Demo), Canada	PHWR/CANDU	Shut down
Rovno-1, Ukraine	PWR/VVER	Operating
Rovno-2, Ukraine	PWR/VVER	Operating
Rovno-3, Ukraine	PWR/VVER	Operating
Rovno-4, Ukraine	PWR/VVER	Under construction
Salem-1, United States	PWR	Operating
Salem-2, United States	PWR	Operating
San Onofre-1 (SONGS-1), United States	PWR	Shut down
San Onofre-2, United States	PWR	Operating
San Onofre-3, United States	PWR	Operating
Santa Maria de Garona, Spain	BWR	Operating
Santa Susana SRE, United States	Na-graphite	Shut down
Santillan-1, Spain	BWR	Suspended indefinitely/Canceled
Sayago-1, Spain	PWR	Suspended indefinitely/Canceled
Schmehausen, Germany	PWR	Suspended indefinitely/Canceled
Seabrook-1, United States	PWR	Operating
Seabrook-2, United States	PWR	Suspended indefinitely/Canceled
Sendai-1, Japan	PWR	Operating
Sendai-2, Japan	PWR	Operating

Sequoyah-1, United States	PWR	Operating
Sequoyah-2, United States	PWR	Operating
Shearon Harris-1, United States	PWR	Operating
Shearon Harris-2, United States	PWR	Suspended indefinitely/Canceled
Shearon Harris-3, United States	PWR	Suspended indefinitely/Canceled
Shearon Harris-4, United States	PWR	Suspended indefinitely/Canceled
Shika-1, Japan	BWR	Operating
Shika-2, Japan	ABWR	Under construction
Shimane-1, Japan	BWR	Operating
Shimane-2, Japan	BWR	Operating
Shippingport, United States	PWR	Shut down
Shoreham, United States	BWR	Shut down
Sinpo-1, Korea DPR (North)	PWR	Under construction
Sinpo-2, Korea DPR (North)	PWR	Planned
Sizewell-A1, United Kingdom	GCR	Operating
Sizewell-A2, United Kingdom	GCR	Operating
Sizewell-B, United Kingdom	PWR	Operating
Smolensk-1, Russian Federation	LWGR/RBMK	Operating
Smolensk-2, Russian Federation	LWGR/RBMK	Operating
Smolensk-3, Russian Federation	LWGR/RBMK	Operating
Smolensk-4, Russian Federation	LWGR/RBMK	Suspended indefinitely/Canceled
South Texas-1, United States	PWR	Operating
South Texas-2, United States	PWR	Operating
South Ukraine-1, Ukraine	PWR/VVER	Operating
South Ukraine-2, Ukraine	PWR/VVER	Operating
South Ukraine-3, Ukraine	PWR/VVER	Operating
South Ukraine-4, Ukraine	PWR/VVER	Suspended indefinitely/Canceled
South Urals-1, Russian Federation	FBR	Suspended indefinitely/Canceled
St. Alban-1, France	PWR	Operating
St. Alban-2, France	PWR	Operating
St. Laurent-A1, France	GCR	Shut down
St. Laurent-A2, France	GCR	Shut down
St. Laurent-B1, France	PWR	Operating
St. Laurent-B2, France	PWR	Operating
St. Lucie-1, United States	PWR	Operating
St. Lucie-2, United States	PWR	Operating
Stade, Germany	PWR	Shut down
Stendal-1, Germany	PWR/VVER	Suspended indefinitely/Canceled
Stendal-2, Germany	PWR/VVER	Suspended indefinitely/Canceled
Super-Phenix, France	FBR	Shut down
Surry-1, United States	PWR	Operating
Surry-2, United States	PWR	Operating
Surry-3, United States	PWR	Suspended indefinitely/Canceled
Surry-4, United States	PWR	Suspended indefinitely/Canceled
Susquehanna-1, United States	BWR	Operating
Susquehanna-2, United States	BWR	Operating

Suzu-1, Japan	ABWR	Suspended indefinitely/Canceled
Suzu-2, Japan	PWR	Suspended indefinitely/Canceled
Takahama-1, Japan	PWR	Operating
Takahama-2, Japan	PWR	Operating
Takahama-3, Japan	PWR	Operating
Takahama-4, Japan	PWR	Operating
Tarapur-1, India	BWR	Operating
Tarapur-2, India	BWR	Operating
Tarapur-3, India	PHWR	Under construction
Tarapur-4, India	PHWR	Under construction
Tatar-1, Russian Federation	PWR/VVER	Suspended indefinitely/Canceled
Tatar-2, Russian Federation	PWR/VVER	Suspended indefinitely/Canceled
Tatar-3, Russian Federation	PWR/VVER	Suspended indefinitely/Canceled
Tatar-4, Russian Federation	PWR/VVER	Suspended indefinitely/Canceled
Temelin-1, Czech Republic	PWR/VVER	Operating
Temelin-2, Czech Republic	PWR/VVER	Operating
Temelin-3, Czech Republic	PWR/VVER	Suspended indefinitely/Canceled
Temelin-4, Czech Republic	PWR/VVER	Suspended indefinitely/Canceled
Three Mile Island-1, United States	PWR	Operating
Three Mile Island-2, United States	PWR	Shut down
THTR-300, Germany	HTGR	Shut down
Tianwan-1, China, Greater	PWR/VVER	Under construction
Tianwan-2, China, Greater	PWR/VVER	Under construction
Tihange-1, Belgium	PWR	Operating
Tihange-2, Belgium	PWR	Operating
Tihange-3, Belgium	PWR	Operating
Tokai-1, Japan	GCR (Magnox)	Shut down
Tokai-2, Japan	BWR	Operating
Tomari-1, Japan	PWR	Operating
Tomari-2, Japan	PWR	Operating
Torness unit A, United Kingdom	AGR	Operating
Torness unit B, United Kingdom	AGR	Operating
Trawsfynydd-1, United Kingdom	GCR (Magnox)	Shut down
Trawsfynydd-2, United Kingdom	GCR (Magnox)	Shut down
Tricastin-1, France	PWR	Operating
Tricastin-2, France	PWR	Operating
Tricastin-3, France	PWR	Operating
Tricastin-4, France	PWR	Operating
Trillo-1, Spain	PWR	Operating
Trillo-2, Spain	PWR	Suspended indefinitely/Canceled
Trino Vercellese, Italy	PWR	Shut down
Trino-1, Italy	PWR	Suspended indefinitely/Canceled
Trino-2, Italy	PWR	Suspended indefinitely/Canceled
Trino-3, Italy	PWR	Suspended indefinitely/Canceled
Trojan, United States	PWR	Shut down
Tsuruga-1, Japan	BWR	Operating

Tsuruga-2, Japan	PWR	Operating
Tullnerfeld, Austria	BWR	Suspended indefinitely/Canceled
Turkey Point-3, United States	PWR	Operating
Turkey Point-4, United States	PWR	Operating
Ulchin-1, Korea RO (South)	PWR	Operating
Ulchin-2, Korea RO (South)	PWR	Operating
Ulchin-3, Korea RO (South)	PWR	Operating
Ulchin-4, Korea RO (South)	PWR	Operating
Ulchin-5, Korea RO (South)	PWR	Under construction
Ulchin-6, Korea RO (South)	PWR	Under construction
Unterweser, Germany	PWR	Operating
Valdecaballeros-1, Spain	BWR	Suspended indefinitely/Canceled
Valdecaballeros-2, Spain	BWR	Suspended indefinitely/Canceled
Vallecitos VBWR, United States	BWR	Shut down
Vandellos-1, Spain	GCR	Shut down
Vandellos-2, Spain	PWR	Operating
Vermont Yankee, United States	BWR	Operating
Virgil C Summer-1, United States	PWR	Operating
Vogtle-1, United States	PWR	Operating
Vogtle-2, United States	PWR	Operating
Vogtle-3, United States	PWR	Suspended indefinitely/Canceled
Vogtle-4, United States	PWR	Suspended indefinitely/Canceled
Volgodonsk-1 (Rostov), Russian Fed.	PWR/VVER	Operating
Volgodonsk-2 (Rostov), Russian Fed.	PWR/VVER	Suspended indefinitely/Canceled
Volgodonsk-3 (Rostov), Russian Fed.	PWR/VVER	Suspended indefinitely/Canceled
Volgodonsk-4 (Rostov), Russian Fed.	PWR/VVER	Suspended indefinitely/Canceled
Waterford-3, United States	PWR	Operating
Watts Bar-1, United States	PWR	Operating
Watts Bar-2, United States	PWR	Suspended indefinitely/Canceled
Windscale WAGR, United Kingdom	GCR (AGR)	Shut down
WNP-1, United States	PWR	Suspended indefinitely/Canceled
WNP-3, United States	PWR	Suspended indefinitely/Canceled
WNP-4, United States	PWR	Suspended indefinitely/Canceled
WNP-5, United States	PWR	Suspended indefinitely/Canceled
Wolf Creek, United States	PWR	Operating
Wolsong-1, Korea RO (South)	PHWR	Operating
Wolsong-2, Korea RO (South)	PHWR	Operating
Wolsong-3, Korea RO (South)	PHWR	Operating
Wolsong-4, Korea RO (South)	PHWR	Operating
Wurgassen, Germany	BWR	Shut down
Wyhl-1, Germany	PWR	Suspended indefinitely/Canceled
Wylfa-1, United Kingdom	GCR	Operating
Wylfa-2, United Kingdom	GCR	Operating
Yankee Rowe, United States	PWR	Shut down
Yellow Creek-1, United States	PWR	Suspended indefinitely/Canceled
Yellow Creek-2, United States	PWR	Suspended indefinitely/Canceled

Yonggwang-1, Korea RO (South)	PWR	Operating
Yonggwang-2, Korea RO (South)	PWR	Operating
Yonggwang-3, Korea RO (South)	PWR	Operating
Yonggwang-4, Korea RO (South)	PWR	Operating
Yonggwang-5, Korea RO (South)	PWR	Operating
Yonggwang-6, Korea RO (South)	PWR	Operating
Zaporozhe-1, Ukraine	PWR/VVER	Operating
Zaporozhe-2, Ukraine	PWR/VVER	Operating
Zaporozhe-3, Ukraine	PWR/VVER	Operating
Zaporozhe-4, Ukraine	PWR/VVER	Operating
Zaporozhe-5, Ukraine	PWR/VVER	Operating
Zaporozhe-6, Ukraine	PWR/VVER	Operating
Zarnowiec-1, Poland	PWR/VVER	Suspended indefinitely/Canceled
Zarnowiec-2, Poland	PWR/VVER	Suspended indefinitely/Canceled
Zarnowiec-3, Poland	PWR/VVER	Suspended indefinitely/Canceled
Zarnowiec-4, Poland	PWR/VVER	Suspended indefinitely/Canceled
Zion-1, United States	PWR	Shut down
Zion-2, United States	PWR	Shut down

LIST OF ACRONYMS

AGR	advanced gas-cooled reactor
AVLIS	atomic vapor laser isotope separation
ABWR	advanced boiling water reactor
BWR	boiling water reactor
CANDU	Canadian deuterium-uranium reactor
DU	depleted uranium
EAR	estimated additional resources
ECCS	emergency core cooling system
EPA	Environmental Protection Agency
EPR	European pressurized reactor
EUP	enriched uranium product
EURATOM	European Atomic Energy Community
FBR	fast breeder reactor
GCR	gas cooled reactor
HAZMAT	Hazardous Material
HEU	highly enriched uranium
HLW	high level waste
HM	heavy metal
HWR	heavy water reactor
IAEA	International Atomic Energy Agency
ILW	intermediate level waste

ISL	in situ leaching
KI	potassium iodide
LEU	low enriched uranium
LLW	low level waste
LOCA	loss of coolant accident
LWGR	light water graphite reactor (RBMK in Russia)
LWR	light water reactor
MAGNOX	magnesium oxide (fuel/reactor)
MLIS	molecular laser isotope separation
MOX	mixed oxide (fuel)
NNWS	non nuclear weapons state
NPP	nuclear power plant
NPT	Non-Proliferation of Nuclear Weapons Treaty
NRC	Nuclear Regulatory Commission (USA)
NWS	nuclear weapons state
PHWR	pressurized heavy water reactor
PUREX	plutonium-uranium reduction extraction
PWR	pressurized water reactor
RAR	reasonably assured resources
RDD	radiological dispersal device
REPU	reprocessed uranium
SILEX	separation of isotopes by laser excitation
SILVA	Séparation Isotopique par Laser de la Vapeur Atomique d'Uranium
SR	speculative resources
SWU	separative work unit
UI	Uranium Institute
UNEP	United Nations Environmental Program
WHO	World Health Organization
WMD	weapon of mass destruction

GLOSSARY

Actinide: An element with atomic number of 89 (actinium) or above.

Activation product: A radioactive isotope of an element (e.g., in the steel of a reactor core) that has been created by neutron bombardment.

ADM (atomic demolition munitions): Small, portable "suitcase nukes" manufactured in the USSR during the Cold War

ALARA (As Low As Reasonably Achievable): Economic and social factors being taken into account, this is the optimization principle of radiation protection.

Alpha particle: A positively charged particle from the nucleus of an atom, emitted during radioactive decay. Alpha particles are helium nuclei, with 2 protons and 2 neutrons.

Atom: A particle of matter which cannot be broken up by chemical means. Atoms have a nucleus consisting of positively charged protons and uncharged neutrons of the same mass. The positive charges on the protons are balanced by a number of negatively charged electrons in motion around the nucleus.

Atom bomb: A nuclear device whose energy comes from the fission of uranium or plutonium.

Background radiation: The naturally occurring ionizing radiation arising from the earth's crust (including radon) or from space radiation that every person is exposed to.

Base load: Those consumers whose demand for electricity demand continuous and does not vary over a twenty-four-hour period. Approximately equivalent to the minimum daily load.

Becquerel: The SI unit of intrinsic radioactivity in a material. One Bq measures one disintegration per second and is thus the activity of a quantity of radioactive material that averages one decay per second. (In practice, GBq or TBq are the common units.)

Beta particle: A particle emitted from an atom during radioactive decay. Beta particles may be either electrons (with negative charge) or positrons (with positive).

Biological shield: A mass of absorbing material (e.g., thick concrete walls) placed around a reactor or radioactive material to reduce the radiation (especially neutrons and gamma rays, respectively) to a level safe for human beings.

Boiling water reactor (BWR): A common type of light water reactor (LWR), wherein water is allowed to boil in the core and generate steam directly into the reactor vessel. (See *PWR*.)

Breed: To form fissile nuclei, usually as a result of neutron capture, possibly followed by radioactive decay.

Breeder reactor: See **Fast breeder reactor** and **Fast neutron reactor**.

Burnable poison: A neutron absorber included in the fuel which progressively disappears and compensates for the loss of reactivity as the fuel is consumed. Gadolinium is commonly used.

Burnup: Measure of thermal energy released by nuclear fuel relative to its mass, typically Gigawatt days per tonne (GWd/tU).

Calandria (in a CANDU reactor): A cylindrical vessel in the reactor that contains the heavy water moderator. It is penetrated from end to end by hundreds of calandria tubes to accommodate the pressure tubes containing the fuel and coolant.

CANDU (Canadian deuterium uranium reactor): moderated and (usually) cooled by heavy water.

CBRN (chemical, biological, radiological, or nuclear): As in weapons at the disposal of terrorist organizations.

Chain reaction: A reaction that stimulates its own repetition, in particular where the neutrons originating from nuclear fission cause an ongoing series of fission reactions.

Cladding: The metal tubes containing oxide fuel pellets in a reactor core.

Concentrate: See **Uranium oxide concentrate**.

Control rods: Devices to absorb neutrons so that the chain reaction in a reactor core may be slowed or stopped by inserting them farther, or accelerated by withdrawing them.

Conversion: Chemical process turning U3O8 into UF6 preparatory to enrichment.

Coolant: The liquid or gas used to transfer heat from the reactor core to the steam generators or directly to the turbines.

Core: The central part of a nuclear reactor containing the fuel elements and any moderator.

Critical mass: The smallest mass of fissile material that will support a self-sustaining chain reaction under specified conditions.

Criticality: Condition of being able to sustain a nuclear chain reaction.

Decay: Disintegration of atomic nuclei resulting in the emission of alpha or beta particles (usually with gamma radiation). Also, the exponential decrease in radioactivity of a material as nuclear disintegrations take place and more stable nuclei are formed.

Decommissioning: Removal of a facility (e.g., reactor) from service; also, subsequent dismantling, safe storage, and making the site available for unrestricted use.

Depleted uranium: Uranium having less than the natural 0.7 percent U-235. As a by-product of enrichment in the fuel cycle, it generally has 0.25 to 0.30 percent U-235, the rest being U-238. Can be blended with highly enriched uranium (e.g., from weapons) to make reactor fuel.

Deuterium: Heavy hydrogen. A stable isotope having one proton and one neutron in the nucleus. It occurs in nature as 1 atom heavy hydrogen to 6,500 atoms normal hydrogen, (Hydrogen atoms contain one proton and no neutrons.)

Dirty bomb: A conventional bomb such as dynamite packaged with radioactive materials.

Element: A chemical substance that cannot be divided into simple substances by chemical means; atomic species with same number of protons.

Dose: The energy absorbed by tissue from ionizing radiation. One gray is one joule per kg, but this is adjusted for the effect of different kinds of radiation, and thus the sievert is the unit of dose equivalent used in setting exposure standards.

Enriched uranium: Uranium in which the proportion of U-235 to U-238 has been increased above the natural 0.7 percent. Reactor-grade uranium is usually enriched to about 3.5 percent U-235; weapons-grade uranium is more than 90 percent U-235.

Enrichment: Physical process of increasing the proportion of U-235 to U-238. See also *SWU*.

Fast breeder reactor (FBR): A fast neutron reactor configured to produce more fissile material than it consumes, using fertile material such as depleted uranium in a blanket around the core.

Fast neutron reactor: A reactor with little or no moderator and hence utilizing fast neutrons. It normally burns plutonium while producing fissile isotopes in fertile material such as depleted uranium (or thorium).

Fertile (of an isotope): Capable of becoming fissile by capturing neutrons, possibly followed by radioactive decay (e.g., U-238, Pu-240).

Fissile (of an isotope): Capable of capturing a slow (thermal) neutron and undergoing nuclear fission (e.g., U-235, U-233, Pu-239).

Fissionable (of an isotope): Capable of undergoing fission: if fissile, by slow neutrons; if fertile, by fast neutrons.

Fission: The splitting of a heavy nucleus into two, accompanied by the release of a relatively large amount of energy and usually one or more neutrons. It may be spontaneous but usually is due to a nucleus absorbing a neutron and thus becoming unstable.

Fission products: Daughter nuclei resulting from either the fission of heavy elements such as uranium or the radioactive decay of those primary daughters. Usually highly radioactive.

Fossil fuel: A fuel based on carbon presumed to be originally from living matter (e.g., coal, oil, gas). Burned with oxygen to yield energy.

Fuel assembly: Structured collection of fuel rods or elements, the unit of fuel in a reactor.

Fuel fabrication: Making reactor fuel assemblies, usually from sintered $UO2$ pellets that are inserted into zircalloy tubes, comprising the fuel rods or elements.

Gamma rays: High energy electromagnetic radiation from the atomic nucleus, virtually identical to X rays.

Genetic mutation: Sudden change in the chromosomal DNA of an individual gene. It may produce inherited changes in descendants. Mutation in some organisms can be made more frequent by irradiation (though this has never been demonstrated in humans).

Giga: One billion units (e.g., gigawatt 109 watts or million kW).

Graphite: Crystalline carbon used in very pure form as a moderator, principally in gas-cooled reactors, but also in Soviet-designed RBMK reactors.

Gray: The SI unit of absorbed radiation dose, one joule per kilogram of tissue.

Greenhouse gases: Radiative gases in the earth's atmosphere which absorb long-wave heat radiation from the earth's surface and re-radiate it, thereby warming the earth. Carbon dioxide and water vapor are the main ones.

Half-life: The period required for half of the atoms of a particular radioactive isotope to decay and become an isotope of another element.

Heavy water: Water containing an elevated concentration of molecules with deuterium ("heavy hydrogen") atoms.

Heavy water reactor (HWR): A reactor which uses heavy water as its moderator (e.g., Canadian CANDU [pressurized HWR or PHWR]).

High-level wastes: Extremely radioactive fission products and transuranic elements (usually other than plutonium) in spent nuclear fuel. They may be separated by reprocessing the spent fuel, or the spent fuel containing them may be regarded as high-level waste.

Highly (or high-) enriched uranium (HEU): Uranium enriched to at least 20 percent U-235. (In weapons, about 90 percent U-235.)

Hydrogen bomb: A nuclear weapon that derives its energy from the fusion of hydrogen. Also known as a thermonuclear weapon.

IAEA: (International Atomic Energy Agency).

In situ leaching (ISL): The recovery by chemical leaching of minerals from porous orebodies without physical excavation. Also known as solution mining.

Ion: An atom that is electrically charged because of loss or gain of electrons.

Ionizing radiation: Radiation (including alpha particles) capable of breaking chemical bonds, thus causing ionization of the matter through which it passes and damage to living tissue.

Irradiate: To subject material to ionizing radiation. Irradiated reactor fuel and components have been subject to neutron irradiation and hence become radioactive themselves.

Isotope: An atomic form of an element having a particular number of neutrons. Different isotopes of an element have the same number of protons but different numbers of neutrons and hence different atomic mass (e.g., U-235, U-238). Some isotopes are unstable and decay to form isotopes of other elements.

Light water: Ordinary water (H_2O), as distinct from heavy water.

Light water reactor (LWR): A common nuclear reactor cooled and usually moderated by ordinary water.

Low-enriched uranium: Uranium enriched to less than 20 percent U-235. (In power reactors, usually 3.5–5.0 percent U-235.)

Megawatt (MW): A unit of power, equal to 106 watts. MWe refers to electric output from a generator, MWt to thermal output from a reactor or heat source (e.g., the gross heat output of a reactor itself, typically three times the MWe figure).

Metal fuels: Natural uranium metal as used in a gas-cooled reactor.

Micro: one millionth of a unit (e.g., microsievert is 10^6 Sv).

Milling: Process by which minerals are extracted from ore, usually at the mine site.

Mixed oxide fuel (MOX): Reactor fuel which consists of both uranium and plutonium oxides, usually about 5 percent Pu, which is the main fissile component.

Moderator: A material such as light or heavy water or graphite used in a reactor to slow down fast neutrons by collision with lighter nuclei so as to expedite further fission.

Natural uranium: Uranium with an isotopic composition as found in nature, containing 99.3 percent U-238, 0.7 percent U-235, and a trace of U-234. Can be used as fuel in heavy water-moderated reactors.

Neutron: An uncharged elementary particle found in the nucleus of every atom except hydrogen. Solitary mobile neutrons traveling at various speeds originate from fission reactions. Slow (thermal) neutrons can in turn readily cause fission in nuclei of fissile isotopes (e.g., U-235, Pu-239, U-233); and fast neutrons can cause fission in nuclei of fertile isotopes (e.g., U-238, Pu-239). Sometimes atomic nuclei simply capture neutrons.

NTARC (National Terror Alert Resource and Information Center).

Nuclear reactor: A device in which a nuclear fission chain reaction occurs under controlled conditions so that the heat yield can be harnessed or the neutron beams utilized. All commercial reactors are thermal reactors, using a moderator to slow down the neutrons.

Nuclear weapon: General term applied to weapons where atoms are split (fission) or where atoms are fused together (fusion). These weapons include atom bombs, hydrogen bombs, thermonuclear bombs, and any other weapons that make use of the releasing of atom particles to create a blast for militaristic purposes.

Oxide fuels: Enriched or natural uranium in the form of the oxide UO_2, used in many types of reactor.

Plutonium: A transuranic element, formed in a nuclear reactor by neutron capture. It has several isotopes, some of which are fissile and some of which undergo spontaneous fission, releasing neutrons. Weapons-grade plutonium is produced in special reactors to give less than 90 percent Pu-239; reactor-grade plutonium contains about 30 percent non-fissile isotopes. About one third of the energy in a light water reactor comes from the fission of Pu-239, and this is the main isotope of value recovered from reprocessing spent fuel.

Pressurized water reactor (PWR): The most common type of light water reactor, it uses water at very high pressure in a primary circuit and steam is formed in a secondary circuit.

Radiation: The emission and propagation of energy by means of electromagnetic waves or particles. (See *Ionizing radiation*.)

Radioactivity: The spontaneous decay of an unstable atomic nucleus, giving rise to the emission of radiation.

Radionuclide: A radioactive isotope of an element.

Radiotoxicity: The adverse health effect of a radionuclide due to its radioactivity.

Radium: A radioactive decay product of uranium often found in uranium ore. It has several radioactive isotopes. Radium-226 decays to radon-222.

Radiological dispersal device (also known as a radiological bomb): The technical term for a dirty bomb.

Radon (Rn): A heavy radioactive gas given off by rocks containing radium (or thorium). Rn-222 is the main isotope.

Radon daughters: Short-lived decay products of radon-222 (i.e., Po-218, Pb-214, Bi-214, Po-214).

RCMP (Royal Canadian Mounted Police).

Reactor pressure vessel: The main steel vessel containing the reactor fuel, moderator and coolant under pressure.

Repository: A permanent disposal place for radioactive wastes.

Reprocessing: Chemical treatment of spent reactor fuel to separate uranium and plutonium from the small quantity of fission product waste products and transuranic elements, leaving a much reduced quantity of high-level waste. (See *Waste, HLW.*)

Separative work unit (SWU): This complex unit is a function of the amount of uranium processed and the degree to which it is enriched (i.e., the extent of increase in the concentration of the U-235 isotope relative to the remainder). Strictly speaking, it's kilogram separative work unit, and it measures the quantity of separative work (indicative of energy used in enrichment) when feed and product quantities are expressed in kilograms. For example, to produce one kilogram of uranium enriched to 3.5 percent U-235 requires 4.3 SWU if the plant is operated at a tails assay 0.30 percent, or 4.8 SWU if the tails assay is 0.25 percent (thereby requiring only 7.0 kg instead of 7.8 kg of natural U feed).

About 100,000 to 120,000 SWU is required to enrich the annual fuel loading for a typical 1000 MWe light water reactor. Enrichment costs are related to electrical energy used. The gaseous diffusion process consumes some 2400 kWh per SWU, while gas centrifuge plants require only about 60 kWh/SWU.

Sievert (Sv): Unit indicating the biological damage caused by radiation. One Joule of beta or gamma radiation absorbed per kilogram of tissue has 1 Sv of biological effect; 1 J/kg of alpha radiation has 20 Sv effect and 1 J/kg of neutrons has 10 Sv effect.

Spent fuel: Fuel assemblies removed from a reactor after several years use.

Stable: Incapable of spontaneous radioactive decay.

Suitcase bomb: A very compact and portable nuclear weapon and could have the dimensions of 60 x 40 x 20 centimeters or 24 x 16 x 8 inches. The smallest possible bomblike object would be a single critical mass of plutonium (or U-233) at maximum density under normal conditions.

Tailings: Ground rock remaining after particular ore minerals (e.g., uranium oxides) are extracted.

Tails: Depleted uranium (See Enriched uranium), with about 0.3 percent U-235.

Thermal reactor: A reactor in which the fission chain reaction is sustained primarily by slow neutrons, hence requiring a moderator (as distinct from Fast neutron reactor).

Transmutation: Changing atoms of one element into those of another by neutron bombardment, causing neutron capture.

Transuranic element: A very heavy element formed artificially by neutron capture and possibly subsequent beta decay(s). Has a higher atomic number than uranium (92). All are radioactive. Neptunium, plutonium, americium, and curium are the best known.

Uranium (U): A mildly radioactive element with two isotopes which are fissile (U-235 and U-233) and two which are fertile (U-238 and U-234). Uranium is the basic fuel of nuclear energy.

Uranium hexafluoride (UF6): A compound of uranium which is a gas above 56°C and is thus a suitable form in which to enrich the uranium.

Uranium oxide concentrate (U3O8): The mixture of uranium oxides produced after milling uranium ore from a mine. Sometimes loosely called yellowcake. It is khaki in color and is usually represented by the empirical formula U3O8. Uranium is sold in this form.

Vitrification: The incorporation of high-level wastes into borosilicate glass, to make up about 14 percent of it by mass. It is designed to immobilize radionuclides in an insoluble matrix ready for disposal.

Waste: High-level waste (HLW) is highly radioactive material arising from nuclear fission. It can be recovered from reprocessing spent fuel, though some countries regard spent fuel itself as HLW. It requires very careful handling, storage and disposal.

Low-level waste (LLW) is mildly radioactive material usually disposed of by incineration and burial.

Yellowcake: Ammonium diuranate, the penultimate uranium compound in U_3O_8 production, but the form in which mine product was sold until about 1970. See also *Uranium oxide concentrate*.

Zircaloy: Zirconium alloy used as a tube to contain uranium oxide fuel pellets in a reactor fuel assembly.

END NOTES

Prologue: New Year's Eve, January 1, 2004.

It turned out: "How U.S. Acted to Foil Dirty Bombers," John Mintz and Susan Schmidt, *Washington Post*, January 8, 2004.

Casually dressed scientists: "U.S. Sends Out 'Dirty Bomb' Patrol," *Washington Post*, January 7, 2004.

[T]he Homeland Security Department: "U.S. Sends Out 'Dirty Bomb' Patrol," *Washington Post*, January 7, 2004.

Batches of radiation: "'Dirty Bomb' Fears: Scientists, Radiation Pagers Dispatched Amid New Year's Bomb Concerns," Pierre Thomas, Mary Walsh and Jason Ryan, ABC NEWS, January 7, 2004.

Department of Energy radiation experts: "U.S. Sends Out 'Dirty Bomb' Patrol," *Washington Post*, January 7, 2004.

sent a Bulletin: "'Dirty Bomb' Fears: Scientists, Radiation Pagers Dispatched Amid New Year's Bomb Concerns," Pierre Thomas, Mary Walsh, and Jason Ryan, ABC NEWS, January 7, 2004.

Secretary of State Colin Powell: "'Dirty Bomb' Fears: Scientists, Radiation Pagers Dispatched Amid New Year's Bomb Concerns," Pierre Thomas, Mary Walsh, and Jason Ryan, ABC NEWS, January 7, 2004.

Introduction

Al-QA`ida continues to: George J. Tenet , Director CIA, "The Worldwide Threat 2004: Challenges in a Changing," Testimony of Director of Central Intelligence, Senate Select Committee on Intelligence, February 24, 2004.

"[T]he continuing threat: George J. Tenet , Director CIA, "The Worldwide Threat 2004: Challenges in a Changing," Testimony of Director of Central Intelligence, Senate Select Committee on Intelligence, February 24, 2004.

Editor's Note

The first act of nuclear terrorism: "U.S. Warns India, Pak Over 'Dirty Bomb' Threat," SIFY.com, SIFY Ltd., India, January 29, 2004.

CHAPTER 1: WHAT IS A DIRTY BOMB?

Osama bin Laden: Tony Karon, "The Dirty Bomb Scenario," *Time* magazine, November 2, 2001.

Western intelligence officials: Tony Karon, "The Dirty Bomb Scenario," *Time* magazine, November 2, 2001.

We have been alerted: Tony Karon, "The Dirty Bomb Scenario," *Time* magazine, November 2, 2001.

is a conventional explosive: Council on Foreign Relations, Terrorism: Questions and Answers: "Dirty Bombs," June 2002.

High explosives inflict: Tom Harris, "Introduction to How Dirty Bombs Work," howstuffworks.com, 2002.

At the levels created: Fact Sheet on Dirty Bombs, U.S. Nuclear Regulatory Commission, March 2003.

However, certain other radioactive materials: Fact Sheet on Dirty Bombs, U.S. Nuclear Regulatory Commission, March 2003.

Dirty nukes are: Mark Thompson, "What is a Dirty Bomb?," *Time* magazine, November 2, 2001.

10,000 people: Mark Thompson, "What is a Dirty Bomb?," *Time* magazine, November 2, 2001.

The long-term destructive force: Tom Harris, "Introduction to How Dirty Bombs Work," howstuffworks.com, 2002.

an ion's electrical charge: Tom Harris, "Introduction to How Dirty Bombs Work," howstuffworks.com, 2002.

years down the road: Tom Harris, "Introduction to How Dirty Bombs Work," howstuffworks.com, 2002.

The extent of local contamination: Fact Sheet on Dirty Bombs, U.S. Nuclear Regulatory Commission, March 2003.

CHAPTER 2: HOW MUCH EXPERTISE DOES IT TAKE TO MAKE A DIRTY BOMB?

No special assembly is required: Council on Foreign Relations, Terrorism: Questions and Answers: "Dirty Bombs," June 2002.

If terrorists wanted: Jim Stewart, "The Mechanics of A 'Dirty Bomb,'" CBS News,

April 23, 2002.

We don't know: Council on Foreign Relations, Terrorism: Questions and Answers: "Dirty Bombs," June 2002.

To make an effective one: Jim Stewart, "The Mechanics of A 'Dirty Bomb,'" CBS News, April 23, 2002.

We don't know if terrorists: Council on Foreign Relations, Terrorism: Questions and Answers: "Dirty Bombs," June 2002.

CHAPTER 3: WHAT'S THE DIFFERENCE BETWEEN A NUCLEAR BOMB AND A DIRTY BOMB?

A dirty bomb is the type of weapon: Dr David Whitehouse, "Making a 'Dirty Bomb'," BBC News Online, June 10, 2002.

Producing either uranium-235: John Ronson, "How to make a Dirty Bomb," *The Guardian*, August 6, 2002.

Operating a nuclear program: Tony Karon, "The Dirty Bomb Scenario," *Time* magazine, November 2, 2001.

Hiroshima and Nagasaki

To understand the difference: Documentation and Diagrams of the Atomic Bomb, Outlaw Labs, January 2, 1996.

The point of total vaporization: Documentation and Diagrams of the Atomic Bomb, Outlaw Labs, January 2, 1996.

On August 9, 1945: Documentation and Diagrams of the Atomic Bomb, Outlaw Labs, January 2, 1996.

A Fission Bomb

There are two main types: Alyn Ware, "How the Bomb Works," Parliamentary Network for Nuclear Disarmament, a project of the Middle Powers Initiative.

Uranium-235 is very difficult to extract: Documentation and Diagrams of the Atomic Bomb, Outlaw Labs, January 2, 1996.

First gaseous diffusion: Documentation and Diagrams of the Atomic Bomb, Outlaw Labs, January 2, 1996.

Depending on the refining process(es): Documentation and Diagrams of the Atomic Bomb, Outlaw Labs, January 2, 1996.

Plutonium is fissionable: Documentation and Diagrams of the Atomic Bomb, Outlaw Labs, January 2, 1996.

A plutonium bomb requires: Documentation and Diagrams of the Atomic Bomb, Outlaw Labs, January 2, 1996.

Fuses are implemented: Documentation and Diagrams of the Atomic Bomb, Outlaw Labs, January 2, 1996.

One mass of uranium is: Alyn Ware, "How the Bomb Works," Parliamentary Network for Nuclear Disarmament, a project of the Middle Powers Initiative.

A Fusion Bomb

In fusion bombs: Alyn Ware, "How the Bomb Works," Parliamentary Network for Nuclear Disarmament, a project of the Middle Powers Initiative.

A Dirty Bomb

A dirty bomb is in no way similar: Fact Sheet on Dirty Bombs, U.S. Nuclear Regulatory Commission, March 2003.

Depending on the sophistication of the bomb: "Terrorism Q&A," Council on Foreign Relations, Cable News Network, 2003.

Radiological attacks: Henry Kelly, Testimony Before the Senate Foreign Relations Committee, "On The Threat of Radiological Attack by Terrorist Groups," March 6, 2002.

While radiological attacks: Henry Kelly, Testimony Before the Senate Foreign Relations Committee, "On The Threat of Radiological Attack by Terrorist Groups," March 6, 2002.

Materials that could easily be lost: Henry Kelly, Testimony Before the Senate Foreign Relations Committee, "On The Threat of Radiological Attack by Terrorist Groups," March 6, 2002.

It is probably more accurate: "Terrorism Q&A," Council on Foreign Relations, Cable News Network, 2003.

Richard Meserve: "Terrorism Q&A," Council on Foreign Relations, Cable News Network, 2003

The effects could also be more long-lasting: "Terrorism Q&A," Council on Foreign Relations, Cable News Network, 2003.

Basically, the principal type of dirty bomb: Fact Sheet on Dirty Bombs, U.S. Nuclear Regulatory Commission, March 2003.

However, certain other radioactive materials: Fact Sheet on Dirty Bombs, U.S. Nuclear Regulatory Commission, March 2003.

A second type of RDD: Fact Sheet on Dirty Bombs, U.S. Nuclear Regulatory Commission, March 2003.

CHAPTER 4: POSSIBLE TYPES OF BOMBS AND DELIVERY METHODS

A Bomb-making Network

found indications of a global bomb-making network: David Johnston, "U.S. Agency Sees Global Network for Bomb Making," *New York Times*, February 22, 2004.

Linkages have been made: David Johnston, "U.S. Agency Sees Global Network for Bomb Making," *New York Times*, February 22, 2004.

Experts . . . have begun to compile: "Bomb-making Network Exposed by U.S.

Probe," worldnetdaily.com, February 22, 2004.

Tedac is a multiagency effort: "Bomb-making Network Exposed by U.S. Probe," worldnetdaily.com, February 22, 2004.

While many intelligence officials: David Johnston, "U.S. Agency Sees Global Network for Bomb Making," *New York Times*, February 22, 2004.

Types of Bombs

TNT

In its refined form: Trinitrotoluene, Wikipedia, 2004.

2,4,6-Trinitrotoluene has been known: 2,4,6-TRINITROTOLUENE(TNT)CAS # 118-96-7U.S. Department of Health and Human Services, Public Health Service Agency for Toxic Substances and Disease Registry.

One might be exposed to: 2,4,6-TRINITROTOLUENE(TNT)CAS # 118-96-7U.S., Department of Health and Human Services, Public Health Service Agency for Toxic Substances and Disease Registry.

Workers involved in: 2,4,6-TRINITROTOLUENE(TNT)CAS # 118-96-7U.S. Department of Health and Human Services, Public Health Service Agency for Toxic Substances and Disease Registry.

Dynamite

75 percent nitroglycerin: "Explosives," *Encyclopaedia Britannica*, 1997.

Ammonium Nitrate

Ammonium nitrate is used: "Bombs, Rockets, and Things That Go BOOM!," totse.com, P.O. Box 5378, Walnut Creek, California 94596.

Other Bombs or Explosive Materials and Terms

"Bombs, Rockets, and Things That Go BOOM!," totse.com, P.O. Box 5378, Walnut Creek, California 94596.

Delivery Systems

Car Bombs

Car Bombs, Wikipedia, 2004.

On April 19, 1995: "The Oklahoma City Bombing," *Indianapolis Star*, October 27, 2001.

A Partial List of Car Bombings: Car Bombs, Wikipedia, 2004.

Suitcases, Luggage, and Backpacks

An explosive RDD: Terrorist CBRN: Materials and Effects, CIA pamphlet, 2003.

Suitcase Nukes

A 'suitcase' bomb: *Suitcase Nukes, National Terror Alert: Terrorism Survival Guide,* Office of Homeland Security, 2003.

portable weapon is a "backpack" bomb: *Suitcase Nukes, National Terror Alert:*

Terrorism Survival Guide, Office of Homeland Security, 2003.

What Are the Effects of a Suitcase Nuke?

According to NTARC: *Suitcase Nukes, National Terror Alert: Terrorism Survival Guide*, Office of Homeland Security, 2003.

Contamination occurs: *Suitcase Nukes, National Terror Alert: Terrorism Survival Guide*, Office of Homeland Security, 2003.

Incorporation of radioactive material: *Suitcase Nukes, National Terror Alert: Terrorism Survival Guide*, Office of Homeland Security, 2003.

Gamma radiation can travel: *Suitcase Nukes, National Terror Alert: Terrorism Survival Guide*, Office of Homeland Security, 2003.

Radiation exposure in the first hour: *Suitcase Nukes, National Terror Alert: Terrorism Survival Guide*, Office of Homeland Security, 2003.

How Real is the Threat of a Suitcase Nuke?

Former Russian Security Council Secretary: Scott Parrish, "Are Suitcase Nukes on the Loose? The Story Behind the Controversy," CNS Reports, November 1997.

The deal is reportedly: "Bush, Blair Warned of bin Laden Nukes," worlddailynet.com, December 14, 2002.

The team's project: "Does al-Qaida Have 20 Suitcase Nukes?," worldnetdaily.com, October 2, 2002.

On February 8, 2004: Nikolai Sokov, in "'Suitcase Nukes': Permanently Lost Luggage," Center for Nonproliferation Studies, February 13, 2004.

Improvised Nuclear Device (IND)

An IND is intended: *Terrorist CBRN: Materials and Effects*, CIA pamphlet, 2003.

CHAPTER 5: CLOSER THAN YOU THINK

"Al-Qaida's apparent interest:" "U.S. Terror Expert Warns of Dirty Bomb," Steven Gutkin, Associated Press, February 11, 2004.

There are millions: "Millions of Dirty Bomb Sources," *New Scientist*, June 25, 2002.

"After September 11:" "U.S. and Russia Hunt for Lost Radioactive Material," *New Scientist*, June 20, 2002.

Finding Radioactive Materials in the U.S.

Significant amounts: Henry Kelly, President, Federation of American Scientists, Before the Senate Foreign Relations Committee, March 6, 2002.

Unfortunately, finding highly radioactive parts: Pierre Thomas, "Radioactive Disappearances, Hundreds of Radioactive Devices Missing, Potential Risk," ABC News, April 11, 2002.

a small, yttrium-90: "Sandia Helps DOE in Control, Tracking of Potential 'Dirty

Bomb' Sources," newswise.com, February 11, 2004.

More than 1,500 radioactive devices: Pierre Thomas, "Radioactive Disappearances, Hundreds of Radioactive Devices Missing, Potential Risk," ABC News, April 11, 2002.

Boy Builds Nuclear Reactor

David was a prodigy: Ken Silverstein, "Tale of the Radio Active Boy Scout," *Harper's*, November 1998.

David learned that a tiny: Ken Silverstein, "Tale of the Radio Active Boy Scout," *Harper's*, November 1998.

Ignoring safety, David mixed: Ken Silverstein, "Tale of the Radio Active Boy Scout," *Harper's*, November 1998.

Abdullah Al Mujahir (a.k.a. Jose Padilla)

While in Afghanistan: "U.S. Authorities Capture 'Dirty Bomb' Suspect," CNN News, June 10, 2002.

Officials suggest al Muhajir: "U.S. Captures 'Dirty Bomb' Suspect," CNN News, June 10, 2002.

It's Not Just the U.S.

There are also some 30,000 old sources: "Millions of Dirty Bomb Sources," *New Scientist*, June 25, 2002.

Up to 40 RCMP cruisers: Jim Bronskill, "Dirty Bomb Fears for Ottawa," Canadian Press, January 14, 2004.

Significant radiological resources: Jim Bronskill, "Dirty Bomb Fears for Ottawa," Canadian Press, January 14, 2004.

After Greece asked" "Agency Helps Greece Defend Against Olympic 'Dirty Bomb' Attack," Global Security Newswire, January 14, 2004.

One does not want: Jon Ronson, "How to Make a Dirty Bomb," *The Guardian* (Manchester), August 6, 2002.

If I was building a dirty bomb: Jon Ronson, "How to Make a Dirty Bomb," *The Guardian* (Manchester), August 6, 2002.

Radiothermal generators: Joby Warrick, "Makings of a 'Dirty Bomb'," *Washington Post*, March 18, 2002.

For terrorists: Joby Warick, "'Dirty Bomb' Warheads Lost," *Washington Post*, December 7, 2003.

There are many sources: Mark Benjamin, "Cohen: 'Dirty Bomb' Might Come from Russia," *Washington Times*, April 23, 2002.

Pakistan

Buhary Syed Abu Tahir: "Pakistan Sold Nuclear Materials to Iran, Libya," Associated Press, MSNBC.com, February 20, 2004.

Border Worries

In October 2003: Bill Gertz, "Al Qaeda Pursued a 'Dirty Bomb,'" *Washington Times*, October 17, 2003.

El Shukrijumah's connection to: Bill Gertz, "Al Qaeda Pursued a 'Dirty Bomb,'" *Washington Times*, October 17, 2003.

We have received: Bill Gertz, "Al Qaeda Pursued a 'Dirty Bomb,'" *Washington Times*, October 17, 2003.

Nuclear Power Plants

The world's 1,300 nuclear facilities: "World's Nuclear Facilities Vulnerable, Warns UN Agency," *New Scientist*, November 1, 2001.

"There is no sanctuary: "World's Nuclear Facilities Vulnerable, Warns UN Agency," *New Scientist*, November 1, 2001.

That same month: "World's Nuclear Facilities Vulnerable, Warns UN Agency," *New Scientist*, November 1, 2001.

CHAPTER 6: THE EFFECTS OF A DIRTY BOMB ATTACK

Casualties

It is possible to kill: Joby Warrick, "Study Raises Projection for 'Dirty Bomb' Toll," *Washington Post*, January 14, 2004.

will be exposed to material: Henry Kelly, President, Federation of American Scientists, "Dirty Bombs: Response to a Threat," Testimony Before the Senate Foreign Relations Committee, March 6, 2002.

Panic

In January 2004: T. K. Malloy, "Report Warns of 'Dirty Bomb' Economic Hit," United Press International, January 14, 2004.

Panic would occur: T. K. Malloy, "Report Warns of 'Dirty Bomb' Economic Hit," United Press International, January 14, 2004.

"The sheer psychological impact: Paul Richter, "Studying 'Dirty Bomb' Scenario," *Los Angeles Times*, April 24, 2002.

On March 6, 2002: Michele Norris and Associated Press, "Weapons of Mass Disruption," ABC News, March 6, 2002.

And John Pike: Michele Norris and Associated Press, "Weapons of Mass Disruption," ABC News, March 6, 2002.

The main purpose of a dirty bomb: Idaho State University, "Dirty Bombs," Radiation Information Network.

We are talking about a weapon: Michele Norris and Associated Press, "Weapons of Mass Disruption," ABC News, March 6, 2002.

Cost

mass casualties: Joby Warrick, "Study Raises Projection for 'Dirty Bomb' Toll," *Washington Post*, January 14, 2004.

The threat of radiological attack: Joby Warrick, "Study Raises Projection for 'Dirty Bomb' Toll," *Washington Post*, January 14, 2004.

equal and perhaps even exceed: Joby Warrick, "Study Raises Projection for 'Dirty Bomb' Toll," *Washington Post*, January 14, 2004.

That would not be the case: T. K. Malloy, "Report Warns of 'Dirty Bomb' Economic Hit," United Press International, January 14, 2004.

CHAPTER 7: WHAT TO DO IN CASE OF A DIRTY BOMB

National Terror Alert: Terrorism Survival Guide, Office of Homeland Security, 2002.

CHAPTER 8: HOW TO PREVENT A DIRTY BOMB

Steps to Cut Off Al Qaeda and Other Terrorist Organizations

We have created: Robert S. Mueller, III, Director, Federal Bureau of Investigation, Annual Conference of the American Muslim Council, Alexandria, Virginia, June 28, 2002 .

There can be no compromise: Robert S. Mueller, III, Director, Federal Bureau of Investigation, Testimony Before the Select Committee on Intelligence of the United States Senate, "War on Terrorism," February 11, 2003.

In his statement: Robert S. Mueller, III, Director, Federal Bureau of Investigation, Testimony Before the Select Committee on Intelligence of the United States Senate, "War on Terrorism," February 11, 2003.

He highlighted the following: Robert S. Mueller, III, Director, Federal Bureau of Investigation, Testimony Before the Select Committee on Intelligence of the United States Senate, "War on Terrorism," February 11, 2003.

Mueller went on: Robert S. Mueller, III, Director, Federal Bureau of Investigation, Testimony Before the Select Committee on Intelligence of the United States Senate, "War on Terrorism," February 11, 2003.

According to Mueller: Robert S. Mueller, III, Director, Federal Bureau of Investigation, Testimony Before the Select Committee on Intelligence of the United States Senate, "War on Terrorism," February 11, 2003.

Securing Existing Radioactive and nuclear Parts and Operations

What is needed: UN International Atomic Energy Agency (IAEA) in Vienna, *New Scientist*, June 2002.

He requested that Congress: Henry Kelly, on the threat of radiological attack by terrorist groups, President Federation of American Scientists, Testimony Before the Senate Foreign Relations Committee, March 6, 2002.

Kelly also insisted: Henry Kelly, on the threat of radiological attack by terrorist groups, President Federation of American Scientists, Testimony Before the Senate Foreign Relations Committee, March 6, 2002.

Kelly also said: Henry Kelly, on the threat of radiological attack by terrorist groups, President Federation of American Scientists, Testimony Before the Senate Foreign Relations Committee, March 6, 2002.

Improving Response Scenarios in Case of Attack

Kelly also pointed out: Henry Kelly, on the threat of radiological attack by terrorist groups, President Federation of American Scientists, Testimony Before the Senate Foreign Relations Committee, March 6, 2002.

Systems capable of detecting: Henry Kelly, on the threat of radiological attack by terrorist groups, President Federation of American Scientists, Testimony Before the Senate Foreign Relations Committee, March 6, 2002.

First responders and hospital personnel: Henry Kelly, on the threat of radiological attack by terrorist groups, President Federation of American Scientists, Testimony Before the Senate Foreign Relations Committee, March 6, 2002.

Updating Equipment

Acquiring sure new products: popularmechanics.com, 2002.

It was the first: popularmechanics.com, 2002.

The private sector: "New Products Offer Radiation Protection Against Dirty Bombs," PRNewswire, January 7, 2004.

The new product: "New Products Offer Radiation Protection Against Dirty Bombs," PRNewswire, January 7, 2004.

RST created a line: "New Products Offer Radiation Protection Against Dirty Bombs," PRNewswire, January 7, 2004.

"We designed this new product line: "New Products Offer Radiation Protection Against Dirty Bombs," PRNewswire, January 7, 2004

Vigilant Security

suspicious package: "'Dirty Bomb' Test Caught U.S. Police Napping," World Headlines, Ireland On-Line, January 13, 2004.

There was not a single: "'Dirty Bomb' Test Caught U.S. Police Napping," World Headlines, Ireland On-Line, January 13, 2004.

The report claimed: "U.S. Police Fail Dirty-Bomb Security Test," *The Scotsman*, January 14, 2004.

Experimenting and Testing "Dirty Bombs"

in an effort to understand: Charles J. Hanley, "U.S., Russia Test 'Dirty Bombs,'" Associated Press, March 14, 2003.

One of the most important findings: Charles J. Hanley, "U.S., Russia Test 'Dirty Bombs,'" Associated Press, March 14, 2003.

focused on tightening protection: Charles J. Hanley, "U.S., Russia Test 'Dirty Bombs,'" Associated Press, March 14, 2003.

A Russian admiral: Charles J. Hanley, "U.S., Russia Test 'Dirty Bombs,'" Associated Press, March 14, 2003.

CHAPTER 9: DIRTY SECRETS, DIRTY BOMBS: U.S. AND RUSSIA

Depleted Uranium Weapons: Why, How, and When – the Benefits

because the radiation levels: "What is a 'Dirty Bomb'?," ABC News, June 10, 2002.

This type of weapon: Robert James Parsons, "Depleted Uranium in Bunker Bombs," *Le Monde Diplomatique*, March 2002.

DU Is Controversial

NATO is only now: Steven Erlanger, "Uranium Furor Puts Kosovars in the Dark Again," *New York Times*, January 12, 2001.

quantities found of uranium 235: Marlise Simons, "Traces of Uranium Isotope Found in U.S. Munitions in Kosovo," *New York Times*, January 17, 2001.

Swiss researchers found: Roger D. Hodge, "Weekly Review," *Harper's* magazine, January 23, 2001.

In the last war: "U.S. to Use Depleted Uranium," BBC News, World Edition, March 18, 2003.

During the Gulf War: Ramsey Clark, "An International Appeal to Ban the Use of Depleted Uranium Weapons" Metal of Dishonor, International Action Center, New York, 1997.

Among the members: Timothy Bancroft-Hinchey, "Evidence That Depleted Uranium Bombs Were Used by USA in 1993. German Defense Minister Says First Case in 1980s," Pravda.Ru, Lisbon, January 23, 2001.

furious about this: Timothy Bancroft-Hinchey, "Evidence That Depleted Uranium Bombs Were Used by USA in 1993. German Defense Minister Says First Case in 1980s," Pravda.Ru, Lisbon, January 23, 2001.

Perhaps the most extraordinary: Elliot Borin, "U.S. Stocking Uranium-Rich Bombs?," wired.com, March 10, 2003.

Gulf War Syndrome

The Committee concludes: Presidential Advisory Committee on Gulf War Veteran's Illnesses, *Final Report*, December 1996.

The chemical toxicity of uranium: Presidential Advisory Committee on Gulf War Veteran's Illnesses, *Final Report*, December 1996.

DU is a leading suspect: Ramsey Clark, "An International Appeal to Ban the Use of Depleted Uranium Weapons," Metal of Dishonor, International Action Center, New York, 1997.

Iraqi doctors have found: John Catalinotto, "U.S. Blocks UN Probe of Depleted Uranium Bombs in Yugoslavia," International Action Center, New York.

In the mid-1990s: Elliot Borin, "U.S. Stocking Uranium-Rich Bombs?," wired.com, March 10, 2003.

A 1991 study: "DU: Cancer as a Weapon," *Counterpunch* magazine, February 5, 2001.

A new study: "DU: Cancer as a Weapon," *Counterpunch* magazine, February 5, 2001.

Since 1990: "DU: Cancer as a Weapon," *Counterpunch* magazine, February 5, 2001.

Balkan Syndrome

Over a dozen have died: Roger D. Hodge, "Weekly Review," *Harper's* magazine, January 9, 2001.

the Portuguese defense minister: Rainer Rupp, "NATO Member Portugal Wants to Withdraw Troops from Kosovo," IAC, October 24, 2000.

APPENDIX

List of Nuclear Facilities Around the World

According to: "Nuclear Q&A," *Bulletin of the Atomic Scientist.*

There are another 550: "Nuclear Q&A," *Bulletin of the Atomic Scientist.*

Of the 429: "Nuclear Q&A," *Bulletin of the Atomic Scientist.*

1. The WNA Reactor Database, World Nuclear Association
   12th Floor, Bowater House West , 114 Knightsbridge, London SW1X 7LJ.
   Website: www.world-nuclear.org

2. IAEA PRIS Database 1: List of World Nuclear Power Reactors in Operation
   (Operating reactors outside of the US as of December 31, 2002)

3. CIA World Book 2003, U.S. Government

GLOSSARY

Some definitions are taken from the World Nuclear Organization.